Kiss Me And Go to Hell

Dare Osatimehin

Copyright © Dare Osatimehin 2014

First published in Great Britain in 2014 by Total Word Publishers

All rights reserved. No part of this publication may be reproduced, stored in a retrieval system or transmitted, in any form, or by any means, electrical, mechanical, photocopying, recording or otherwise without the prior written permission of the publisher or a licence permitting restricted copying.

A catalogue record for this book is available from the British Library.

All bible references and quotes are from the King James Version

ISBN 978-0-9565259-0-1

DEDICATION

To my lovely wife
Oluwarantimi
And my wonderful children
Demilade
Nathan
Iyanu-Oluwa
I love being yours
I love you all being mine
I love all of us being children of the most High God

CONTENTS

Forward 9

Preface 11

1 Who Is a Christian? 13

2 God is a God of Blessing 19

3 God is a Covenant Keeping God 23

4 God Has a School of Waiting and Patience 27

5 God Does Not Give an Impossible command 31

6 The Plain Truth About Alcohol 35

7 The Bible and The Wine 39

8 Lot's Family and a Shameful End 49

9 What Will You Give Back To God 61

10 The Source and Strength of The Triumphant Life ... 69

11 Living to Please The Lord 79

12 The Surrendered Consecrated Life 89

13 The Spirit Controlled Life 99

14 The Spirit's Ministry in The Believer's Life 109

15 Fallacy of The Doctrine of Predestination 119

16 The Great White Throne of Judgement 129

17 Free and Never To Be Bound 137

18 Alcohol Anonymous 143

19 Classification of Wine 153

20 Alcohol and Wine 161

A Prayer of Salvation 169

Bible Abbreviations 171

About The Author 173

Another Book By The Author 174

ACKNOWLEDGEMENT

A special thanks to my friend and co-labourer in the vineyard, Mrs. Busola Adesanya-Yusuf; for your patience and sacrifice for the many hours of typing and editing this manuscript. Your eagle eyes made a lot of difference;
To my sons in the faith, your heart-searching questions and the brain teasers kept me on my toes to work harder.
And to my erratic friend, Tayo Utomi for being part of this.
I couldn't have done this without you all.

FORWARD

The Holy Bible affirms, "The Lord gave the Word, Great was the company of those that proclaimed (published) it"-Psalm 68:11. Kiss me and Go to Hell simply put is a lucid dossier on spiritual uprightness, drawn from the personal experience of the author, an erudite scholar & spiritual guru, Pastor Dare Osatimehin, a non-compromising, committed combatant of the true word of God and of Christ's crusade & Kingdom. This book is a must read for all fellow Citizens of Heaven while demonstrating judicious practical applications.
  Pastor Samuel Oludare Agboola -Christ Dominion

In Kiss me and Go to Hell, Pastor Dare Osatimehin, wrote from the heart, and as a man is, so is his writing. Dare demonstrates his love for his neighbour by his burning desire that everyone should make heaven. Therefore he warns of the evil consequences of the abuse and misuse of alcohol. He catalogues events from as far back as early creation period that have changed the course of human history due to alcohol. However, in doing so he has not failed to show appreciation for the use of alcohol as food, drug and chemical reagent. "Kiss me and Go to Hell" is a must read for everyone in the hope that the warning expressed in it is heeded.
  Rev. George O. Baptist -President, Equipping The Saints (ETS), African Missions

We live in a time when many are lost without a clear direction in regards to their lives, more so are many, who are bound by destructive habits that stifle their progress, and ultimately frustrate their destiny. During this time, God will always raise up men that will declare God's truth from His word, which will liberate and strengthen the spirit of a man to pursue God diligently and from a pure heart. Dr Dare Osatimehin is one of such men, who has a great desire to share God's truth in its purest sense, and this book "Kiss me and Go To Hell" is definitely one that is filled with authenticity, inspired by the Holy Spirit. For anyone wanting to experience and work in Jesus' promise of liberty, this book will not go amiss.

Pastor Abraham Oluleke Rufai -Power House International Ministries London

PREFACE

One of the greatest decisions a Christian has to make in this present evil world is the choice of what to eat, drink, wear and who to associate with. There are so many that have a form of godliness but deny the power there of. From such the bible clearly says we should turn away. Living a Christ-like life in this Christ-less society and most especially with so many saints in the church and sinners outside, one wonders if one is a lone voice in the wilderness.

Where does the believer stand and what does he or she believe on the issue of alcohol and wine? "All things are lawful for me, but not all things are helpful; all things are lawful for me, but not all things edify", so says the Holy Scripture.

The government of this world are making billions from alcohol; yet they are killing millions from alcohol and alcohol related diseases. When will this touch the heart of the children of God? After all, if all men go to hell who cares? We should care.

Kiss me and go to hell is a book that takes an in-depth look at the biblical stand on alcohol and wine. From Genesis to Revelation., the Holy Bible makes it clear on what the children of God should believe and do.

Should one drink wine?
What about the small percentages of the mixed wines in our stores and supermarkets today?
What did Jesus turn water into at the miracle in Cana of Galilee?

What type of wine does the bible command us to tithe and bring to His house?
Why did Apostle Paul encourage his 'son' Tim. to drink a little wine?
What should a Christian be intoxicated with?
Are there individuals and families destroyed by wine in the bible?
How long will the children of God and especially you halt between two opinions?

These and more are what this book is all about. You will also discover the strength to live a wine and alcohol free life and be another 'Lily in the valley'. Yes, you can and will make a difference. You can and will be free, never to be bound again by the chains of alcohol and wine.

God bless you really good.

1
WHO IS A CHRISTIAN?

The man who expects to go to heaven should take the trouble to learn what route will get him there

People can come into church and profess Christianity; it does not matter, as long as they don't practice it. We are in a generation where everyone call themselves children of God. The word born again has been abused by the generation of today. The teaching of Jesus in John 3 was to Nicodemus who was already a teacher of the Law, yet he didn't know the way to the kingdom of God. Who needs to be born again today? I am very sure you know the answer. The church leaders, Pastors, Teachers, Evangelist and all the category of church title holders that their positions and titles in the church are more important than their position in the Kingdom of God need to be born again. We all seem to forget that those positions which are highly 'exalted among men are an abomination before God'. Jesus said, "except ye be converted and be as little children, you shall in no way enter the Kingdom of God." The devil wants you to come into the knowledge of the faith, provided you don't practice it.

You can say you serve God; it does not really matter as long as you don't practice it. The more you practice what you have been taught, the more you will have impact in the world. The less you practice, the less your impact will be outside in the world. It's better to be hated for what you are than to be loved for what you are not. Be real with yourselves, be practical, do not be a saint in the church and a sinner outside. Let all hate you for who you are, rather than love you for who you are not. Let your Christianity be real for all to see.

Who then is a Christian? A Christian is one who has personally accepted Jesus Christ as his Lord and Saviour. He has carried his cross and is following his master. We do know as well that a Christian is who he is, by what he does with what he has; his position, wealth and popularity do not distract him from his Lord and Saviour.

Truth and the Theory of the Truth

Truth is the natural stimulus of the mind, especially truth that reveals moral obligation.

When the devil begins to deceive an individual, he makes him believe the theory of the truth more than the truth itself. The truth as Jesus said it is, "I am the way the truth and the life, nobody goes to the father, except by me." That is the truth. The theory of the truth asks, "you mean there is only one way - how about other religions? How about such and such doctrines?" This is the theory of the truth. The truth is all sinners will go to hell. Those who do not accept Jesus Christ as their personal Lord and Saviour will be lost in eternity.

The truth is that there are 'books open before God' and there is only one 'Book of the Lamb', the book of Life where all the names of the true children of God are written, and whosoever's name is not found in this Book of Life will live eternity in the lake of fire that burns with sulphur and brimstone. The theory of the truth asks, "how can the God of love create billions of people and destroy them later, He must be unjust." The theory of the truth makes people forget about God's provision for the way of salvation. When asked to describe the truth, please, leave elegance for the tailor.

Gen. 9:1 - And God blessed Noah and his sons, and said unto them, be fruitful, and multiply, and replenish the earth
Gen. 9:2 - And the fear of you and the dread of you shall be upon every beast of the earth, and upon every fowl of the air, upon all that moveth upon the earth, and upon all the fishes of the sea; into your hand are they delivered
Gen. 9:3 - Every moving thing that liveth shall be meat for you; even as the green herb have I given you all things
Gen. 9:4 - But flesh with the life thereof, which is the blood thereof, shall ye not eat
Gen. 9:5 - And surely your blood of your lives will I require; at the hand of every beast will I require it, and at the hand of man; at the hand of every man's brother will I require the life of man
Gen. 9:6 - Whoso sheddeth a man's blood; by man shall his blood be shed: for in the image of God made he man
Gen. 9:7 - And you, be ye fruitful, and multiply; bring forth abundantly in the earth, and multiply therein
Gen. 9:8 - And God spake unto Noah, and to his sons with him, saying
Gen. 9:9 - And I, behold, I establish my covenant with you and with your seed after you
Gen. 9:10 - And with every living creature that is with you, of the fowl, of the cattle, and of every beast of the earth with you; from all that go out of the ark, to every beast of the earth
Gen. 9:11 - And I will establish my covenant with you; neither shall all flesh be cut off any more by the waters of a flood; neither shall there anymore be a flood to destroy the earth
Gen. 9:12 - And God said, this is the token of the covenant which I make between me and you and every living creature that is with you, for perpetual generations
Gen. 9:13 - I do set my bow in the cloud and it shall be for a token of a covenant between me and the earth
Gen. 9:14 - And it shall come to pass, when I bring a cloud over the earth, that the bow shall be seen in the cloud
Gen. 9:15 - And I will remember my covenant, which is between me and you and every living creature of all flesh; and

the waters shall no more become a flood to destroy all flesh

Gen. 9:16 - And the bow shall be in the cloud; and I will look upon it, that I may remember the everlasting covenant between God and every living creature of all flesh that is upon the earth

Gen. 9:17 - And God said unto Noah, This is the token of the covenant, which I have established between me and all flesh that is upon the earth

Gen. 9:18 - And the sons of Noah that went forth of the ark were Shem, and Ham, and Japheth: and Ham is the father of Canaan.

Gen. 9:19 - These are the three sons of Noah: and of them was the whole earth overspread

Gen. 9:20 - And Noah began to be an husbandman, and he planted a vineyard:

Gen. 9:21 - And he drank of the wine, and was drunken; and he was uncovered within his tent

Gen. 9:22 - And Ham, the father of Canaan, saw the nakedness of his father, and told his two brethren without

Gen 9:23 - And Shem and Japheth took a garment, and laid it upon both their shoulders, and went backward, and covered the nakedness of their father; and their faces were backward, and they saw not their father's nakedness

Gen. 9:24 - And Noah awoke from his wine, and knew what his younger son had done unto him

Gen. 9:25 - And he said, Cursed be Canaan; a servant of servants shall he be unto his brethren

Gen. 9:26 - And he said, Blessed be the LORD God of Shem; and Canaan shall be his servant

Gen. 9:27 - God shall enlarge Japheth, and he shall dwell in the tents of Shem; and Canaan shall be his servant

Gen. 9:28 - And Noah lived after the flood three hundred and fifty years

Gen. 9:29 - And all the days of Noah were nine hundred and fifty years: and he died.

Are there few to be saved?

Eternity is a journey. We are journeying from here to heaven. When we started the journey is very important but what we see in the journey cannot be the same. My experience of the journey will be very different from yours, but the ultimate is that we are going to end up in only one place which is called Heaven. The way you start, how you enter the journey does not really matter, either by crawling or by somersaulting, you are in the journey. But where you are going to end is the most important thing. Look at history and study your bible; so many people started the journey, only few eventually made it to the end. Jesus said, "Are there few to be saved?" And the people said, "this is a hard saying, who can bear this?" Study from Genesis to Revelation and you will see all the people that started the journey and the ones that couldn't make it.

I remember when we newly gave our lives to Jesus Christ several years ago. How many were we then? Thousands! But today how many are still in the race? Some of my friends whom we started the race together and were doing everything together, even becoming pastors now have two wives. Yet they continue to preach and I often wonder which Bible they are preaching from. That is part of what you see in the journey. The direction you are facing has a lot to do with your destination. Of course, starting the journey and being able to end it depends on God, but most importantly it rests in your hands. There is no point in me deceiving myself about serving God. If I want to serve Him, I will serve Him, and if not, I will simply stay somewhere else. The same goes for you; don't deceive yourself, serve God if you want to serve Him or look for something else to do.

"So God blessed Noah and his sons". I want to lead you to a place where I will leave you into the hands of God that you will make a choice and determine what and how your own journey is going to be. I have no doubt in my mind and I believe what God has said that He will bless you.

Dare Osatimehin

2

GOD IS A GOD OF BLESSING

*No man is without a divinely-appointed task and
divinely bestowed strength adequately for its fulfilment*

I have no doubt in my mind and I believe what God has said, that He will bless His people and His Church. There is no doubt in my mind, because we are called by the name of The Most High God. We pray all the time on your behalf even when you are not aware, so I have no doubt in my mind that God will bless you. However I have a problem; what are you going to do with the blessing when God has blessed you? I can't do anything about it, since you are the only one that knows. When God finally releases the things you are praying about, what will become of you. When you read the bible passage further, you will see, "So God blessed Noah and his sons and said to them be fruitful and multiply and fill the earth."

That was God's blessing for Noah and his family after the first generation had been destroyed. What eventually became of this new generation God blessed is what we don't know, but as we go along you will see what Noah eventually turned into in the Bible. Even nowadays, when people are praying for God's blessing and God eventually settles them, what they turn into is often a cause for concern.

God blessed Noah very well, not because he was righteous, neither because he was so prayerful, nor because he was a perfect man. If you read Gen. chapter 6 from verse 8, the Bible says "but Noah found Grace in the eyes of the lord … Noah was a just man - perfect in his generation, Noah walked with God." The original word used here as perfect was used thirty nine times in the Old Testament and does not mean to live righteously, rather it talks about when you are appreciating God with an offering – like a lamb or a sheep and the sheep does not have any blemish. Noah was very handsome in God's presence, he had no blemish. Apart from that, from the first generation, the only pure Adamic stock that was still remaining was Noah and his family. All the others had been corrupted through the former antediluvian world. The Bible says Noah was perfect. This does not mean Noah was a very righteous person, rather because he was from the pure stock of Adam and God had to preserve His seed through Adam since that was the provision for the coming of Jesus Christ. So God blessed the family of Noah who had not corrupted themselves.

Looking at Gen. Chapter 9, you will see that there was the first Adam, who is the Adam we see in Genesis and there is the second Adam who is Jesus Christ. In as much as you are a child of God, there is no doubt in my mind that my God is going to bless you; not because of what you have done, but because of the blessings of the second Adam, Jesus Christ. As long as you are a Christian and you have accepted Jesus Christ as your Lord and Saviour, God MUST bless you and He will bless you. That is very sure. What I don't know and what I can't predict is what you will turn into when God has finished blessing you.

Let's jump to verse 8, where we see God's blessing upon Noah. In verse 7, the bible says, "as for you, be fruitful and multiply, bring forth abundantly in the earth," and in verse 8, "and God spoke to Noah and to his sons with him, saying "and as for me, behold I establish my covenant with you and with your descendants after you and with every living creature that is with you; the birds, and every beast with you; of all that go out of the ark every beast of the earth thus I establish my covenant with you, never again shall any flesh be cut off by the waters of the flood, never again shall there be a flood to destroy the earth." And God said, "this is the sign of the covenant which I make between me and you and every living creature that is with you for a perpetual generation." God is a covenant keeping God. When God has promised something, He is going to do it, He might postpone it till another next generation if you err against His covenant, but on God's side He is not going to deny making a promise or a covenant concerning you. That is why I am sure there is a covenant that cannot fail between you and God if you are His child.

Dare Osatimehin

3

GOD IS A COVENANT KEEPING GOD

He who does not understand your silence will definitely not understand your words

On God's part He will not break His covenant because He is a covenant keeping God. Although there are categories of covenants, I am talking about the common, general covenant that you receive when you give your life to Jesus Christ. Eventually, the problem is centred around how you are going to keep your own end of the covenant so that you won't break it because the power to keep your part of the covenant does not depend on God, but on you. When God made a covenant with Noah, and said, "Noah, listen I have destroyed all that I have created, apart from you, your family and whatever is in the ark. Now, no matter how many days it rains and even if everywhere is flooded, I have made a sign with you that never in this life will I use flood to destroy the whole earth again. This is a token of my covenant; no matter how much it rains, I will send a rainbow, when you see the rainbow, I will remember my covenant with you and your family and based on that behalf, the whole generation of human life will be preserved."

Gen. 9:11 - And I will establish my covenant with you; neither shall all flesh be cut off any more by the waters of a flood; neither shall there anymore be a flood to destroy the earth
Gen. 9:12 - And God said, this is the token of the covenant which I make between me and you and every living creature that is with you, for perpetual generations
Gen. 9:13 - I do set my bow in the cloud and it shall be for a token of a covenant between me and the earth.
Gen. 9:14 - And it shall come to pass, when I bring a cloud

over the earth, that the bow shall be seen in the cloud:
Gen 9:15 - And I will remember my covenant, which is between me and you and every living creature of all flesh; and the waters shall no more become a flood to destroy all flesh.
Gen. 9:16 - And the bow shall be in the cloud; and I will look upon it, that I may remember the everlasting covenant between God and every living creature of all flesh that is upon the earth.
Gen. 9:17 - And God said unto Noah, This is the token of the covenant, which I have established between me and all flesh that is upon the earth.

What a wonderful God, what a great privilege for God to make a covenant with an individual and through him the whole world was to be blessed. You can trace this to the book of Luke, Chapter 3 verse 36, "Which was the son of Cainan, which was the son of Arphaxad, which was the son of Sem, which was the son of Noe, which was the son of Lamech." There is a need to understand that before the time of Noah there was only one generation on the earth. There were no other nations, there were no races and no tribes, and there was only one generation.

Now God said for you to multiply and fill the earth, there is something I am going to do; I am going to bring nations and generations out of you so that the whole world will again become populated. It was after the flood, that nations and races sprang up through Noah in the way we have in the whole world today. There will be no racism, tribalism, sectarianisms, sexism, in heaven. All the inhabitants are called God's children. Please be sure you are there. I am sure that through you the whole world will be blessed. There is no doubt in my mind what God has implanted in you will be a blessing to you and generations to come. However, I don't know what your generation will turn into after you.
Gen. Chapter 9, verse 18 says, "Now the sons of Noah who went out of the ark were Shem, Ham and Japheth and Ham was the father of Canaan." These three were the sons of Noah

and from them the whole earth was populated through nations and tribes. That was God's part of the covenant and He stood by it and fulfilled it. But eventually what every generation will do on their own part is what no man can predict. God knew it, but Noah himself did not know it.

I need to make it clear here that with God, there is no confusion for He knows the end from the beginning. If you read this verse carefully, you will note that Shem, the middle son, is always mentioned first because it was through him that the Messiah would come. Japheth was the eldest. Gen. 10:21 says, "Unto Shem also, the father of all the children of Eber, the brother of Japheth the elder, even to him were children born." 1Chron. 1:4-5, "Noah, Shem, Ham, and Japheth. The sons of Japheth; Gomer, and Magog, and Madai, and Javan, and Tubal, and Meshech, and Tiras." Ham was the youngest, Gen. 9:22-24. "And Ham, the father of Canaan, saw the nakedness of his father, and told his two brethren without". Gen. 9:23, "And Shem and Japheth took a garment, and laid it upon both their shoulders, and went backward, and covered the nakedness of their father; and their faces were backward, and they saw not their father's nakedness. Gen. 9:24, "And Noah awoke from his wine, and knew what his younger son had done unto him." Verse 20, "And Noah began to be a farmer and he planted a vineyard and he drank of the wine and was drunk and became uncovered in his tent".

It is not wrong for God to bless us. Noah was the first owner of a vineyard in the bible. After preaching for one hundred and twenty years, there was no convert apart from him and his three children and their wives. When he was preaching, there was no church, no bible, no congregation, yet he was not discouraged. God confirmed Noah's message, that He would send rain and the whole world will be judged and destroyed. The people knew that in their generation it had never rained, so when Noah said God had spoken to him and that He would send rain, the people reminded him that from the days of their great grandfathers it had never rained. The suggestion was that something was wrong with him and medical attention should be sought.

Based on God's commandment, Noah started preaching and building the ark while noting to take the animals two by two (male and female) with him. God confirmed Noah's message after years of preaching. He opened the face of the deep and there was rain on earth for forty days. "God opened the curtains of heaven and the waters from the deep came up. The flooding was on the surface of the earth for one hundred and fifty days."

4

GOD HAS A SCHOOL OF WAITING AND PATIENCE

It may be difficult to wait on the Lord, but it is worse to wish you had waited

Gen. 7:10 - And it came to pass after seven days that the waters of the flood were on the earth.

After Noah and his family entered the ark, they were in it for seven days waiting for the rain to come. You can begin to imagine the reproach, ridicule, insult, mockery and everything that the world would have been hurling at them during that time. Like Noah, you've got to know the Lord you serve is able to bring to fulfilment all that He has promised, otherwise you will easily buckle under any flimsy situation. Let your feet stand firmly on the solid rock that never fails because God will test and try all that is inside of you before fulfilling whatever good thing He has promised you.

As we know more of God, the more God takes us and teaches us things that only Him can teach us. There is a school called patience and waiting where God's children are taught and schooled in the art of waiting patiently. In this school, there is no worry and anxiety. Just like David in the book of Psalms waited patiently, so we are to do likewise today, nothing less is required of us. Under the grace of today, we are expected to even do more because we are under a better covenant and understanding powered by the indwelling power of the Holy Spirit.

Psalm 40:1 - I waited patiently for Jehovah; and he inclined unto me, and heard my cry.
Psalm 40:2 - And he brought me up out of the pit of destruction, out of the miry clay, and set my feet upon a rock;

he hath established my goings
Psalm 40:3 - And he hath put a new song in my mouth, praise unto our God. Many shall see it, and fear, and shall confide in Jehovah
Psalm 40:4 - Blessed is the man that hath made Jehovah his confidence, and turneth not to the proud, and to such as turn aside to lies
Psalm 40:5 - Thou, O Jehovah my God, hast multiplied thy marvellous works, and thy thoughts toward us: they cannot be reckoned up in order unto thee; would I declare and speak them, they are more than can be numbered

David waited (past tense) patiently and the following happened to him:
- He inclined unto me
- Heard my cry
- He brought me up out of the pit of destruction
- He brought me out of the miry clay
- He set my feet upon a rock
- He hath established my goings
- He hath put a new song in my mouth
- He taught me the praise unto our God
- Many shall see it, and fear, and shall confide in Jehovah (after my graduation from God's school of waiting and patience)

It is better to have waited for God than to wish you had waited. Good things happen to those who wait. Stop moving faster than your shoes. Patience is waiting without worry. Worry is the interest paid on trouble before trouble comes. Worry is like sitting on a rocking chair; no matter how many times you rock, you get nowhere. Worry does not empty today of its sorrows and troubles; it only empties tomorrow of its strength. Leave all in the care of our mighty God and He will take good care of you.

Matt. 6:34 - Take therefore no thought for the morrow: for the morrow shall take thought for the things of itself. Sufficient unto the day is the evil thereof.

One songwriter captured the words of our Lord in the following words of his song:

I'm Only Human, I'm Just A Man

Lord, help me believe
In what I could be
And all that I am,
Just show me the stairway
That I have to climb.
Lord, for my sake
Teach me to take
One day at a time.

One day at a time, Lord Jesus,
That's all I'm asking from you.
Just give me the strength
To do every day what I have to do.
Yesterday is gone, Lord Jesus;
And tomorrow may never be mine.
Lord, help me today, show me the way,
One day at a time.

One of the great secret of living a happy, healthy, holy and fruitful life is living without worry about the past and without anxiety concerning the future. The true child of God settles the past with God. He has confessed the sins of the past and he has been forgiven. Now he shuts out the past and counts everything belonging to the past dead, buried and never to rise again. Locking the past behind an iron door, he throws the key of remembrance away! The future is yet unborn, so he leaves that with God until it comes. Leaving the past and future with God, he summons all grace received, strength and courage to face the challenges of each day.

Leave tomorrow with God and His good foresight.

"Take therefore no thought for the morrow." It is an unnecessary distraction to worry or be anxious about tomorrow. There are men who waste their last hours on earth fretting over a tomorrow they never see! If we are preserved till tomorrow, will it not bring with it tomorrow's God? What good can your worry do? It does not empty tomorrow of its problems and trials, but it empties today of its strength and comfort. Worrying about tomorrow does not enable you to escape future troubles, it only weakens you and makes you unfit to cope with those challenges when tomorrow eventually comes.

Worrying about tomorrow often leads to hurtful imagination which produces wrong thinking and self-induced negative prophecies and tormenting fear. Don't try to cross the bridge before you get to it, but cheerfully carry the cross of today and leave the future to God. He will be there before you get there. When tomorrow dawns and its door swings open, the power and promises of God will be waiting for you to welcome you to a new day. "As thy days, so shall thy strength be." (Deut. 33:25).

5

GOD DOES NOT GIVE AN IMPOSSIBLE COMMAND

We ask God to promote us, and when He does, we congratulate ourselves upon our successes

How was Noah able to travel the world and get the animals? You need to watch the discovery channel to know the extent of types of animals in the sea and land. How marvellous and wonderful God is in His awesome creation.

Let us read the bible account in Genesis.

Gen. 6:19 - And of every living thing of all flesh, two of every sort shalt thou bring into the ark, to keep them alive with thee; they shall be male and female
Gen. 6:20 - Of fowls after their kind, and of cattle after their kind, of every creeping thing of the earth after his kind, two of every sort shall come unto thee, to keep them alive

It is unimaginable to try and think of the unsearchable riches, wisdom and power of the creator of heaven and earth. He does not give and will never give an impossible command. The God that I know will never ask from us what He has not provided for us. Whatever commandment He wants us to obey, He knows we have enough grace to obey it. God will not give us a task that is not within our human ability to accomplish. Quite often we tend to see our inability and forget about God's divine ability. There should be a lifting of your faith as you read this because God in His infinite mercy has given unto all His children all they need to become what God Himself wants them to become. Increase your faith, move up higher, for with our God all things are possible. It was not Noah that was looking everywhere for the creatures to make their way to the ark. God Himself spoke to the creatures themselves; two of every kind. With a divine general global positioning system and satellite navigation, they all knew Noah's address and location and they all came in their different and unique species and submitted themselves to Noah, waiting patiently to take up their new home in the Ark. What a wonderful God.

When you are in a divine covenant relationship with God, all things work in your favour. As the creature of God located Noah's ark, I pronounce today that your business, husband, wife, children, job, opportunities, health and connections will locate you in Jesus name. All we have to do is to position ourselves where God wants us to be.

The animals did not eat each other. God's plan and purpose is for all of His children to live together in harmony, to live and have a taste of heaven here on earth. This is possible, and it will be done. God preserved Noah and his family inside the ark for one year and seventeen days when the whole generation was destroyed. God honoured him so much that he was the first person to build an altar after the flood and God accepted his offering. The first cathedral was built by him.

Around this time Noah had spent over 600 years of his life building a reputation. Referring to verse 20, "then Noah began to be a farmer and he planted a vineyard, then he drank of the wine and was drunk and became uncovered in his tent." Noah became the first alcoholic that ever lived; he became the first man to curse his own children in the new generation. What he had built for six hundred years, his reputation was destroyed by one single act. Reputation is built by many acts but destroyed by a single act.

Once a reputation is destroyed it can be repaired, but the

whole world will point at that one point where the reputation was destroyed. We read how God blessed Noah, but we still remember him as the first alcoholic and drunkard of the new era, despite God's investment.

Dare Osatimehin

6

THE PLAIN TRUTH ABOUT ALCOHOL

He who is not grateful for the good things he has would not be happy with what he wishes he had

One thing we have learnt from past civilisation is that it is filled with ingratitude. Despite all that God had invested in people, what they came back to pay Him with was misbehaviour and disobedience to His commandments. What are you going to pay God back with despite His investment in you? It's not in God's hands, it's in your hands.

Noah spent the last three hundred years of his life, living a life God never planned for him. It's not today that alcohol has been the problem of the whole world; the first generation was destroyed and the second one came up and just that single act destroyed it. If that could happen, then we are in slight danger of also losing it the way those other guys lost it.

Gen. Chapter 9, verse 22 tells how Ham the father of Canaan saw the nakedness of his father, and told his two brothers outside. But Shem and Japheth took a piece of cloth and laid it on both their shoulders, using it to cover the nakedness of their father, they turned their faces away and did not see their father's nakedness. "Noah awoke from his wine and knew what his young son had done to him and he said, "cursed be Canaan, the servant of servants he shall be to his brethren." And he said, "blessed be the Lord the God of Shem, May Canaan be his servant, may God enlarge Japheth and may he dwell in the tents of Shem and may Canaan be his servant." What a good father! And Noah lived after the flood three hundred and fifty years. The days of Noah were nine hundred and fifty years when he died.

It is not in this world that sin pays its people with good wages and it will never pay them. A bite of sin leaves a bitter after taste. I find it difficult to express in words and context what I wish to express here to you, but as you see what eventually happened to Canaan, Shem and Japheth, I believe you will understand me better.

If alcohol has been the problem of the world, forget about the world then and think about our world today and how alcohol is contributing to most crimes and accidents on our roads. We witness the fact that billions of money is being spent fighting alcoholism everywhere. If the government is fighting this and the church is supporting them, it would be more effective, but church members are still becoming drunkards. That is a problem. If alcohol destroyed the first world, what will happen to this generation? This cannot be predicted.

Of course, God will bless His children, because faithful is He who has promised, and He will do it, but what the children will turn into is what we cannot guarantee. Think about what God has done for you; think about what you have repaid him with. When people have problems; looking for children or jobs or demons are chasing them, they will start sleeping in church. But once the problem is solved, the pastor will call their homes and they won't bother to return the call. The usual response is "Pastor we are very busy." You were not busy before, and nobody had to run after you because you were poor and broke then. But now, you have houses and children and everything is good and rosy and you don't have time for fellowship anymore. What you will turn into remains to be seen. When you were not as rich as this, your wife was so nice to you and you to her, but now you are established, she has become who you can beat and talk to anyhow.

I have been to so many marriage and birthday celebrations among church people and I often wondered what would happen at the next one I will attend. It is only a few parties that I don't see different tables for Christians and for sinners. Even the big people in church will bring alcohol and sit comfortably as if it's normal despite the fact that alcohol destroyed the first world as we have discovered in the bible.

Dare Osatimehin

7
THE BIBLE AND WINE

Learn as though you were to live forever; live as though you were to die tomorrow

The Hebrew word used for wine in the scriptures is Yayin and it was generally used in the Bible on many occasions. To rightly know the true meaning and usage, we need to pay attention to some facts.

Twelve facts about Hebrew Yayin
Wine in the broadest sense, including all types both fermented and unfermented.

1. When fermented makes drunk (Gen.9:21-24; 19:32-35; 1 Sam.25:37; 2 Samuel.13:28; Esther 1:10; Psalm 104:15; Prov. 23:30; Isaiah 5:11).

2. Yayin refers to wine when newly made and before fermentation (Isaiah 16:10; Jer. 48:33, compare Matthew 9:17; Mark 2:22; John 2:3-10).

3. Permitted in moderation under the law of Moses (Deut. 14:23, 26; 16:13; 18:4).

4. Nazarites forbidden to drink it (Num. 6: 1-21).

5. Used in drink offerings to God (Exodus 29:40; Lev 23:13; Numbers 15:5-10; 28:14).

6. Distinct from strong drink (Heb.az, strong, vehement; and shathah, to imbibe; drink, Lev.10:9; Deut.14:26:29:6; Judges 13:4,7,14; 1 Sam 1:15, compare Luke 1.15).

7. Makes eye red (Gen. 49:12).

8. Is a mocker (Prov. 20:1)

9. Not to be used when red (Prov.23:31)

10. Not for Kings (Prov. 31:4)

11. Often mixed with spices and other drinks (Prov. 9:2; 23:30; Songs of Solomon 8:2).

12. Offered by Melchizedek to Abraham (Gen. 14:18)

The golden nugget here is that Noah drank from fermented wine as seen in (1) above and Jesus turned water into wine- newly made wine before fermentation as seen in (2) above.

Ten other Hebrew words for wine

1. Tiyrosh was used thirty nine times compared to Yayin one hundred and thirty six times, and means newly made wine from grapes. It is the word used for prosperity under the term corn and wine (Gen 27:28, 37; Deut. 7:13; 11: 14; 18:4; 28:51; 33:28; 2Ki.18:32; 2Chr.31:5). It is translated with new (Neh. 10:37, 39 ; 13:5, 12; Prov. 3 :10 ; Isaiah 24:7; 65:8; Hosea. 4:11; 9:2; Joel 1 :10 ; 3:18; Haggai. 1:11; Zech. 9:17) and with sweet (Micah.6:15). Tiyrosh was the wine to be tithed (Deut. 12:17; 14:23). Yayin is never spoken of as being tithed. It generally refers to older grape juice, and God required the first fruits or newly made wine as well as the first fruits of other crops and the firstborn of animals and man (Ex. 13:2, 15; 23:16-19; 34:26). Juice of grapes is called wine when still in the cluster (Isaiah. 65:8).

Yayin and Tiyrosh are the main words for wine.

2. Enab - grape drink (Hosea. 3:1).

3. Aciyc - fresh grape juice (Isaiah 49:26; Joel 1:5; 3:18; Amos 9:13).

4. Shekar - an intoxicant; alcoholic liquor: strong drink (Num. 28:7; Deut.14:25-26). It was made from barley, honey, and dates.

5. Yeqeb -juice from the lower wine vat into which the wine drains to purify it when first pressed in the press.(Deut. 16:13).

6. Chemer - wine of the grapes as fermenting: pure red wine. (Isaiah. 27:2).

7. Chamar - red wine (Ezra 6:9; 7:22; Daniel 5:1, 4, 23).

8. Gath - treading out grapes (Neh. 13:15). Translated as winepress (Judges 6:11; Isaiah 63:3) and winefat (Isaiah 63:2).

9. Cobe - wine; mixed wine (Isaiah 1:22).

10. Mamcak - mixed wine with water or spices (Proverbs 23:30).

Bible references to wine in the New Testament

In the New Testament, a lot of references were made to wine. As you look closely at some of them, you will be clearer and more definite on which stand to take and what to believe in.

- New or newly made wine as grape juice (Matt. 9:17;

Mark 2:22; Luke 9:37-39), the new wine of Acts 2:13 refers to sweet wine. The Greek word is sometimes used in Greek literature as fermented wine.
- Mixed wine (Mark 15:23).
- Contrasted with strong drink (Luke 1:15).
- Used as medicine (Luke 10:34).
- Jesus made wine (John 2:3-10; 4:46).
- Advise against wine for Christians (Romans 14:21).
- Warning against drunkenness by wine (Eph. 5:18), excess of wine (1 Peter4:3), and one not be given to wine (1 Tim. 3:3,8; Titus 1:7; 2:3).
- Timothy was advised to use a little wine for his infirmity (1 Tim. 5:23).
- Used figuratively (Rev. 14:8,10; 16:19; 17:2; 18:3).
- Ruthless destruction of it forbidden (Rev. 6:6).

It must be remembered that the word wine is used for both fermented and unfermented drink in scriptures, therefore the absolute meaning cannot always be determined and applied in every one of the above scriptural passages. Knowing that the bible speaks of the juice of grapes as wine while it is still in the cluster (Isaiah 65:8), and calls it new wine when it is just pressed out of the grapes makes it difficult to decide in every case whether the reference is to that which is fermented or unfermented. However, one should always remember the warning in the bible about drunkards. "One thing is certain: a drunkard shall not inherit the kingdom of God. (Luke 21:34; Romans 13:13; 1Cor. 6:9-11; Gal. 5:19-21).

The Book of Isaiah, Chapter 1, verse 2 says, "Hear, O heavens, and give ear, O earth, for the Lord has spoken I have nourished and brought up children, and they have rebelled against me. The ox knoweth his owner, and the ass his master's crib; but Israel doth not know, my people doth not consider. Alas, o nation, a people laden with iniquity a brood of evil doers, children who are corrupters and they have forsaken the Lord, they have provoked the Holy One of Israel unto anger, they are gone away backward. Why should you be stricken again, you will revolt more and more. The whole head is sick and the whole heart faints."

If you were ever stopped when coming from parties, where will you end if you were already above the alcohol limit? Prov. Chapter 20; verse 1 says, "Wine is a mocker, strong drink is a brawler and whosoever is led astray by it is a foolish person."

Prov. 21:17 - He who loves pleasure will be a poor man, he who loves wine and oil shall not be rich….. like a serpent and stinks like a viper, your eyes will see strange things and your heart will utter perverse things. Useless jokes will come out, you will cherish naked women. Yes you will be like one who lies down in the midst of the sea, or as he that lieth upon the top of the mast. Saying, they have stricken me, and I was not sick, they have beaten me, and I felt it not; when shall I awake that I may seek another drink.

Prov. 31:4 - It is not for kings, O Lemuel, it is not for kings to drink wine; nor for princes strong drink; lest they drink and forget the law, and pervert the judgment of any of the afflicted. Give strong drink unto him that is ready to perish, and wine unto those that be of heavy hearts.

Prov. 23:29 - Who hath woe? Who hath sorrow? Who hath contentions? Who hath babbling? Who hath wounds without cause? Who hath redness of eyes?
Prov. 23:30 - They that tarry long at the wine; they that go to seek mixed wine
Prov. 23:31 - Look not thou upon the wine when it is red, when it giveth his colour in the cup, when it moveth itself aright
Prov. 23:32 - At the last it biteth like a serpent, and stingeth like an adder
Prov. 23:33 - Thine eyes shall behold strange women and thine

heart shall utter perverse things
Prov. 23:34 - Yea, thou shalt be as he that lieth down in the midst of the sea, or as he that lieth upon the top of a mast
Prov. 23:35 - They have stricken me, shalt thou say, and I was not sick; they have beaten me, and I felt it not: when shall I awake? I will seek it yet again.

Isaiah 5:11 - Woe to those who rise early in the morning that they may follow intoxicating drinks, who continue until night, till wine inflames them.

Isaiah 28:1 - Woe to the crown of pride, to the drunkards of Ephraim, whose glorious beauty is a fading flower, which are on the head of the fat valleys of them that are overcome with wine. Verse 7 - But they also have erred through wine and through strong drink, are out of the way; the priest and the prophet have erred through strong drink, they are swallowed up of wine, they are out of the way through strong drink; they err in vision, they stumble in judgement.

Isaiah 28:8 - For all tables are full of vomit and filthiness, so that there is no place clean.

"Yea also, because he transgresses by wine, he is a proud man, neither keepeth at home, who enlargeth his desire." *Kiss this and go to hell.* "And he is like death and cannot be satisfied, and gathers to himself all nations, and heaps unto him all peoples."

Hab. 2:15 - Woe to him who gives drink to his neighbour, pressing him to your bottle that you may look upon his nakedness
Hab. 2:16 - Thou art filled with shame for glory: drink thou also, and let thy foreskin be uncovered: the cup of the LORD'S right hand shall be turned unto thee, and shameful spewing shall be on thy glory.

Why does the Scripture forbid drinking of intoxicating wine?

God does not perform miracles that will lead people into captivity. His power is compatible with his holiness. Jesus did not turn water into intoxicating wine for men to drink and continue in sin. Some people erroneously misinterpret 'wine' in our text to be alcohol. It needs to be clarified that there are two types of wine produced from grapefruit or pomegranate in the Middle East; unfermented and fermented wine.

The unfermented wine is non-alcoholic fruit juice. This is very nutritious food for the body. It was used as:
- Beverage at festivals (Esther 1:7; 5:6; Daniel 5:1-4; John 2:3)
- Drink-offerings in the temple service (Exodus 20:26; Numbers 15:4-10)
- Part of the "first-fruits" (Deut. 18:4)
- To celebrate the Passover (Numbers 23:13)
- And by extension, the Lord's Supper (Matt. 26:27-29).

This kind of good wine cannot make one 'bad' or 'abnormal'. Would Christ turn water into alcoholic wine for guests to drink, get intoxicated and disrupt activities at the marriage? God forbid!

Intake of fermented, alcoholic wine that intoxicates is unarguably sinful as it results in degrading behaviours (Gen. 9:20; 19:31-36; 1 Samuel 25:36-37; 2 Samuel 13:28; 1 Kings 20:12-21; Esther 1:10-11; Daniel 5:23; Rev. 17:2).

Miseries, woes, errors, folly and wickedness describe those who take alcoholic wine (Prov. 23:29-35; Isaiah 5:22; 28:1-7; 5:11, 12; 56:12; Hosea 4:11; Joel 3:3; Amos 6:6). And these are not the descriptive qualities of the redeemed children of God. God forbids His children from taking alcohol (Lev. 10:9; Numbers 6:3; 1 Samuel 1:14; Prov. 23:31; 31:4-5; 1 Tim. 3:3; 1 Cor. 6:9-10; Rev. 21: 8, 27). To take or not to take alcoholic wine but give others attracts a curse (Hab. 2:15).

Paul's advice to Timothy in 1Tim. 5:23, "drink no longer only water, but use a little wine on account of thy stomach and thy frequent illnesses." This advice from Paul to Timothy to use a little wine for his stomach's sake and often infirmities adds another dimension to this issue. In Paul's exhortation on personal duty to his son him, he pointed out that an ascetic practice that adversely affected health would not keep a person pure (verse 22). Impure water supplies often made wine a common beverage in those days. Timothy may have been totally abstaining from this beverage, possibly as an ascetic practice. Understandably, alcohol is medicinal. It is a basic constituent of most drugs we use from day to day. Timothy was asked to use a measure of it (Yayin-fermented wine) to cure his stomach's trouble. Those who misconstrue this statement as licence to drink alcoholic wine obey their flesh and attract God's displeasure on them. Medically, the use of drugs without a doctor's recommendation is drug abuse, and punishable in the law court.

What are the reasons for Christ performing miracles? Christ's first miracle of turning water into wine was performed to show forth the glory of God. Besides, miracles, signs and wonders attest to the potency of the power of God. Genuine miracles from Christ also draw sinners unto God so they can receive the greatest of all miracles – the salvation of their souls. Divine manifestation also makes the believer to exercise absolute trust in the sovereignty of God. As a result of the miracle, "his disciples believed on him," (John 2:11).

The Devil's Strategy

The devil is willing for a person to confess Christianity, as long as he does not practise it

1 Peter 5:8 - Be sober, be vigilant; because your adversary the

devil, as a roaring lion, walketh about, seeking whom he may devour. What a warning this is for us all as children of God. Even though the devil seeks whom he may devour, the bible does not say the devil devours all he seeks. The choice is still yours if you will allow the devil to win this battle over you. If I were you, I will sing this chorus and song and make the words living and practical in me.

I will never let the devil win the battle
I will never compromise with him
Though he may try me within
Yes, he may try me without
I will never, I will never let the devil win

The question is, do you know what the devil does? The devil could not stand against Noah's message because it had heavenly backing. The devil cannot stand against God preserving humanity. Since the devil could not convert Noah and stop his message, he decided to corrupt him and he did.

Be on your guard and watch out:
- If the devil cannot convert you, he will try to corrupt you.
- If the devil cannot prevent you, he will try to persecute you.
- If the devil cannot deny you, he will try to deactivate you.
- If the devil cannot promote you, he will try to pollute you.
- If the devil cannot destroy you, he will try to demote you.
- If the devil cannot enslave you, he will try to entice you.
- If the devil cannot stop you, he will put stumbling blocks in your way.
- If the devil cannot remove you, he will try to redirect

you.

Noah was corrupted, persecuted, enticed and alcohol became the stumbling block on his way.

8

LOT'S FAMILY AND A SHAMEFUL END

I'd rather walk in the dark with God than walk alone in the light;
I'd rather walk with Him by faith than walk alone by sight

Gen. 19:29 - And it came to pass, when God destroyed the cities of the plain, that God remembered Abraham, and sent Lot out of the midst of the overthrow, when he overthrew the cities in the which Lot dwelt
Gen. 19:30 - And Lot went up out of Zoar, and dwelt in the mountain, and his two daughters with him; for he feared to dwell in Zoar: and he dwelt in a cave, he and his two daughters
Gen. 19:31 - And the firstborn said unto the younger, Our father is old, and there is not a man in the earth to come in unto us after the manner of all the earth
Gen. 19:32 - Come, let us make our father drink wine, and we will lie with him, that we may preserve seed of our father
Gen. 19:33 - And they made their father drink wine that night: and the firstborn went in, and lay with her father; and he perceived not when she lay down, nor when she arose
Gen.19:34 - And it came to pass on the morrow, that the firstborn said unto the younger, Behold, I lay yester night with my father: let us make him drink wine this night also; and go thou in, and lie with him, that we may preserve seed of our father
Gen. 19:35 - And they made their father drink wine that night also: and the younger arose, and lay with him; and he perceived not when she lay down, nor when she arose
Gen. 19:36 - Thus were both the daughters of Lot with child by their father

Gen. 19:37 - And the firstborn bare a son, and called his name Moab: the same is the father of the Moabites unto this day.
Gen. 19:38 - And the younger, she also bare a son, and called his name Benammi: the same is the father of the children of Ammon unto this day.

Lot had benefited so much from his association with the man of God, Prophet Abraham. Even though God did not call Lot, he enjoyed the benefit of associating with a covenant child of God. I sincerely wish that our association with God will benefit others. The challenge we all face is how to handle the blessings of God. The two daughters of Lot said there was no man on earth to marry them so as to have children. That verse actually means that there was no man of their own family and kindred to marry them. They were actually afraid to marry the men of Zoar who had been marked for destruction along with Sodom for homosexuality. They forgot about the family of Abraham.

What a useless excuse to commit whoredom. You can make your choices in life, but you cannot control the consequences of those choices you have made. No doubt, Lot's daughters had seen many made drunk in the drinking places of Sodom. Needless to say that having lived in such a city where they were surrounded by wickedness in its vilest form and kind, these same daughters now betrayed the confidence of their own father who had chosen such a place for their home. They were out of Sodom, but Sodom was still inside them.

How about you my beloved brethren? God has called us out of the world, we must all endeavour to get the world out from inside of us, for where the heart is, there the treasure is laid and stored. It is good to note with all clarity that excuses might be reasonable but they are not excusable. Lot himself did not learn how to drink to become a drunkard in the cave; he must have been drinking while he was in Sodom. He must have had several episodes of drunkenness in the presence of his children, so his daughters grew up knowing his weakness.

If you are a careless and carefree parent, start paying good attention to the quality of life that you are living and portraying in the presence of your children. Any inadequacies that you might notice now, I appeal to you in the name of the Lord that you work on them and correct them, for you never know when and how you will pay for them in the future. How careless did Lot become that he was living in a cave with two mature and grown up daughters. Permit me to ask you to please cover you nakedness in the presence of your children.

The daughters of Lot had two sons for their father from what we can only term 'a one night stand' today. A bite at sin leaves a bitter aftertaste in your mouth. Lot's single night of shame resulted in two nations, Moab and Ben-ammi being born by his two daughters.

Begotten in shame both sons had a shameful history (Num. 22-24; Deut. 2:9, 19; Judges 3:11; I Samuel 11; 2 Samuel 8:10).

Deut. 2:9 - And the LORD said unto me, "Distress not the Moabites, neither contend with them in battle: for I will not give thee of their land for a possession; because I have given Ar unto the children of Lot for a possession.

I Samuel 11:1 - Then Nahash the Ammonite came up, and encamped against Jabesh-gilead: and all the men of Jabesh said unto Nahash, Make a covenant with us, and we will serve thee
1Samuel 11:2 - And Nahash the Ammonite answered them, on this condition will I make a covenant with you, that I may thrust out all your right eyes, and lay it for a reproach upon all Israel
1Samuel 11:3 - And the elders of Jabesh said unto him, Give us seven days' respite that we may send messengers unto all the coasts of Israel: and then, if there be no man to save us, we will come out to thee.

1Samuel 11:4 - Then came the messengers to Gibeah of Saul, and told the tidings in the ears of the people: and all the people lifted up their voices, and wept

1Samuel 11:5 -And, behold, Saul came after the herd out of the field; and Saul said, What ailed the people that they weep? And they told him the tidings of the men of Jabesh

1Samuel 11:6 - And the Spirit of God came upon Saul when he heard those tidings, and his anger was kindled greatly

1Samuel 11:7 - And he took a yoke of oxen, and hewed them in pieces, and sent them throughout all the coasts of Israel by the hands of messengers, saying, Whosoever cometh not forth after Saul and after Samuel, so shall it be done unto his oxen. And the fear of the LORD fell on the people, and they came out with one consent

1Samuel 11:8 - And when he numbered them in Bezek, the children of Israel were three hundred thousand, and the men of Judah thirty thousand

1Samuel 11:9 - And they said unto the messengers that came, Thus shall ye say unto the men of Jabesh-gilead, tomorrow, by that time the sun be hot, ye shall have help. And the messengers came and shewed it to the men of Jabesh; and they were glad

1Samuel 11:10 - Therefore the men of Jabesh said, tomorrow we will come out unto you, and ye shall do with us all that seemed good unto you

1Samuel 11:11 - And it was so on the morrow, that Saul put the people in three companies; and they came into the midst of the host in the morning watch, and slew the Ammonites until the heat of the day: and it came to pass, that they which remained were scattered, so that two of them were not left together.

Both were cursed (Deut. 23: 3; Neh. 13:1, 23-25; Isaiah. 11:14; Zeph. 2).

Deut. 23:3- An Ammonite or Moabite shall not enter into the congregation of the LORD; even to their tenth generation shall they not enter into the congregation of the LORD for ever.

Neh. 13:1 - On that day they read in the book of Moses in the audience of the people; and therein was found written, that the Ammonite and the Moabite should not come into the congregation of God for ever
Neh. 13:2 - Because they met not the children of Israel with bread and with water, but hired Balaam against them, that he should curse them: howbeit our God turned the curse into a blessing
Neh. 13:23 - In those days also saw I Jews that had married wives of Ashdod, of Ammon, and of Moab
Neh. 13:24 - And their children spake half in the speech of Ashdod, and could not speak in the Jews' language, but according to the language of each people
Neh. 13:25 - And I contended with them, and cursed them, and smote certain of them, and plucked off their hair, and made them swear by God, saying, Ye shall not give your daughters unto their sons, nor take their daughters unto your sons, or for yourselves

Isaiah 11:14 - But they shall fly upon the shoulders of the Philistines toward the west; they shall spoil them of the east together: they shall lay their hand upon Edom and Moab; and the children of Ammon shall obey them.

Take note that this was the first sin of incest in the bible; a man having sex with his children. This was all due to alcohol. When you are under the influence of alcohol, high and intoxicated, you will do those things that you will not ordinarily do. The Ammonites and the Moabites are the people of whom God spoke to the Israelites about, commanding them when they got to Canaan to destroy all their generations because they were the children of Alcohol and Incest.

Cases of incest in the bible

- Lot and his two daughters (Gen.19: 31-36)
- Abraham and Sarah (Gen. 20: 12-13)
- Nahor and Milcah (Gen.11:29)
- Reuben and Bilhah (Gen. 35:22; 49:4)
- Judah and Tamar (Gen. 38:16-18; 1Chron. 2:4)
- Amram and Jochebed (Exodus 6:20)
- Amnon and Tamar (2 Samuel 13:14)
- Absalom and David's wives (2 Samuel 16:21)
- Herod (Matt. 14:3-4; Mark 6:17-18; Luke 3:19)
- A Corinthian (I Cor. 5:1-2)

It must be well understood that while all these would have been condemned by the law of Moses (as we have in Lev. 18:6-18; 20:11-21; Deut. 22:30; 27:20-23), such marriages as that of Abraham and his half-sister, and that of Nahor and Milcah before the law, were excusable during the period in which they took place as God was populating the new world in His divine order.

Acts 17:30 - And the times of this ignorance God winked at; but now commanded all men everywhere to repent.

Lev. 18:6 - None of you shall approach to any that is near of kin to him, to uncover their nakedness: I am the LORD

Lev. 18:7 - The nakedness of thy father, or the nakedness of thy mother, shalt thou not uncover: she is thy mother; thou shalt not uncover her nakedness

Lev. 18:8 - The nakedness of thy father's wife shalt thou not uncover: it is thy father's nakedness

Lev. 18:9 - The nakedness of thy sister, the daughter of thy father, or daughter of thy mother, whether she be born at home, or born abroad, even their nakedness thou shalt not uncover

Lev. 18:10 - The nakedness of thy son's daughter, or of thy daughter's daughter, even their nakedness thou shalt not uncover: for theirs is thine own nakedness

Lev. 18:11 - The nakedness of thy father's wife's daughter, begotten of thy father, she is thy sister, thou shalt not uncover her nakedness

Lev. 18:12 - Thou shalt not uncover the nakedness of thy father's sister: she is thy father's near kinswoman

Lev. 18:13 - Thou shalt not uncover the nakedness of thy mother's sister: for she is thy mother's near kinswoman

Lev. 18:14 -Thou shalt not uncover the nakedness of thy father's brother, thou shalt not approach to his wife: she is thine aunt

Lev. 18:15 -Thou shalt not uncover the nakedness of thy daughter in law: she is thy son's wife; thou shalt not uncover her nakedness

Lev. 18:16 - Thou shalt not uncover the nakedness of thy brother's wife: it is thy brother's nakedness

Lev. 18:17 - Thou shalt not uncover the nakedness of a woman and her daughter, neither shalt thou take her son's daughter, or her daughter's daughter, to uncover her nakedness; for they are her near kinswomen: it is wickedness

Lev. 18:18 - Neither shalt thou take a wife to her sister, to vex her, to uncover her nakedness, beside the other in her life time

Lev. 18:19 - Also thou shalt not approach unto a woman to uncover her nakedness, as long as she is put apart for her uncleanness

Lev. 18:20 - Moreover thou shalt not lie carnally with thy neighbour's wife, to defile thyself with her

Lev. 18:21 - And thou shalt not let any of thy seed pass through the fire to Molech, neither shalt thou profane the name of thy God: I am the LORD

Lev. 18:22 - Thou shalt not lie with mankind, as with womankind: it is abomination

Lev 18:23 - Neither shalt thou lie with any beast to defile thyself therewith: neither shall any woman stand before a beast to lie down thereto: it is confusion

Lev. 18:24 - Defile not ye yourselves in any of these things: for in all these the nations are defiled which I cast out before you
Lev. 18:25 - And the land is defiled: therefore I do visit the iniquity thereof upon it, and the land itself vomiteth out her inhabitants
Lev. 18:26 - Ye shall therefore keep my statutes and my judgments, and shall not commit any of these abominations; neither any of your own nation, nor any stranger that sojourneth among you.

Are you for sale? You need to answer this question; are you for sale? If you are for sale, what's the price on your head?

- Achan offered himself for a wedge and a garment and he was lost.
- Judas offered himself for just 30 pieces of silver and he was lost.
- Ahab offered himself for a piece of vineyard and was lost.
- Samson offered himself for Delilah's lap and bosom, and he was lost.
- How about Noah? He offered himself for sale for some wine and he was lost.
- Esau offered himself for a small portion of porridge and lost his birth right and was lost.
- Lot offered himself for a pint of wine, committed incest and God said all his generations must be destroyed.
- Demas offered himself for the love of 'this present world' and was lost.
- Ananias and Sapphira offered themselves for deceit and were lost.
- Balaam offered himself to gain wages of unrighteousness and he was lost.
- The young prophet offered himself for delay and disobedience from taking heed to God's instruction and he was lost in eternity.

Kiss Me and Go To Hell

Are you for sale? If you answer is yes, how much? What is your discounted price? Is it buy one, get one free or half discounted price? Is that how cheap you really are? For how much will alcohol buy you?

Have You Counted The Cost?

1. There's a line that is drawn by rejecting our Lord,
   Where the call of His Spirit is lost,
   And you hurry along with the pleasure-mad throng -
   Have you counted, have you counted the cost?

Chorus:
Have you counted the cost, if your soul should be lost?
Though you gain the whole world for your own?
Even now it may be that the line you have crossed,
Have you counted, have you counted the cost?

2. You may barter your hope of eternity's morn,
   For a moment of joy at the most,
   For the glitter of sin and the things it will win-
   Have you counted, have you counted the cost?

3. While the door of His mercy is open to you,
   Ere the depth of His love you exhaust,
   Won't you come and be healed, won't you whisper, I yield
   I have counted, I have counted, the cost.

Yield Not To Temptation

1. Yield not to temptation,
   For yielding is sin;
   Each victory will help you,
   Some other to win;
   Fight manfully onward,
   Dark passions subdue;

Look ever to Jesus,
He'll carry you through.

Chorus:
Ask the Saviour to help you;
Comfort, Strengthen, and keep you;
He is willing to aid you,
He will carry you through.

2. Shun evil companions,
   Bad language disdain;
   God's name holds in reverence,
   Nor take it in vain;
   Be thoughtful and earnest,
   Kind-hearted and true;
   Look ever to Jesus,
   He'll carry you through.

3. To him that ov'ercometh,
   God giveth a crown;
   Thro' faith we will conquer,
   Though often cast down;
   He who is our Saviour,
   Our strength will renew;
   Look ever to Jesus,
   He'll carry you through.

There's A Great Day Coming

1. There's a great day coming,
   A great day coming,
   There's a great day coming by and by;
   When the saints and the sinners shall
   Be parted right and left,
   Are you ready for that day to come?

Chorus:
Are you ready? Are you ready?
Are you ready for the judgment day?
Are you ready? Are you ready?
For the judgment day?

2. There's a bright day coming,
   A bright day coming,
   There's a bright day coming by and by;
   But its brightness shall only come
   To them that love the Lord,
   Are you ready for that day to come?

3. There's a sad day coming,
   A sad day coming,
   There's a sad day coming by and by;
   When the sinner shall hear his doom,
   "Depart, I know ye not,"
   Are you ready for that day to come?

Where Shall I be?

1. When judgment day is drawing nigh, where shall I be?
   When God the works of men shall try, where shall I be?
   When east and west the fire shall roll, where shall I be?
   How will it be with my poor soul? Where shall I be?

Chorus:
O where shall I be when the first trumpet sounds,
O where shall I be when it sounds so loud?
When it sounds so loud as to wake up the dead?
O where shall I be when it sounds?

2. When wicked men his wrath shall see, where shall I be?
   And to the rocks and mountains flee, where shall I be?
   When hills and mountains flee away, where shall I be?

When all the works of men decay, where shall I be?

3. When heav'n and earth as some great scroll, Where shall I be?
Shall from God's angry presence roll, where shall I be?
When all the saints redeem'd shall stand, where shall I be?
Forever blest at God's right hand, where shall I be?

4. All trouble done, all conflict past, where shall I be?
And old Apollyon slain at last, where shall I be?
When Christ shall reign from shore to shore, where shall I be?
And peace abide forevermore, where shall I be?

9

WHAT WILL YOU GIVE BACK TO GOD?

1Chron. 29:14 Isaiah 55:1-2
No Christian leader can be truly rich who is selfish

1 Chron. 29:14 - But who am I, and what is my people, that we should be able to offer so willingly after this sort? For all things come of Thee, and of Thine own have we given Thee.

Isaiah 55:1 - Ho, every one that thirsteth, come ye to the waters, and he that hath no money; come ye, buy, and eat; yea, come, buy wine and milk without money and without price
Isaiah 55:2 - Wherefore do ye spend money for that which is not bread? And your labour for that which satisfieth not? Hearken diligently unto me, and eat ye that which is good, and let your soul delight itself in fatness.

To be able to offer anything to God is a perfect mystery. Consecration is a miracle of grace. "All things come of Thee, and of Thine own have we given Thee." In these words there are four very precious thoughts I want to try and make clear to you:
1. God is the Owner of all, and gives all to us.
2. We have nothing but what we receive, but everything we need we may receive from God.
3. It is our privilege and honour to give back to God what we receive from Him.
4. God has double joy in His possessions when He receives back from us what He gave.

And when I apply this to my life - to my body, to my wealth, property and to my whole being with all its powers-then I understand what consecration ought to be.

1. It is the glory of God, and His very nature, to be always GIVING. God is the owner of all. There is no power, no riches, no goodness, no love, outside of God. It is the very nature of God that He does not live for Himself, but for His creatures. His is a love that always delights to give. Here we come to the first step in consecration. I must see that everything I have is given by Him; I must learn to believe in God as the great Owner and Giver of all. Let me hold that fast. I have nothing but what actually and definitely belongs to God. Just as much as people say, "this money in my purse belongs to me," so God is the Proprietor of all. It is His and His only. And it is His life and delight to be always giving. Oh, take that precious thought-there is nothing that God has that He does not want to give. It is His nature, and therefore when God asks you anything, He would have given it first Himself. Never be afraid whatever God asks, for God only asks what is His own. The Possessor, and Owner, and Giver of all! This is our God. You can apply this to yourself and your powers to all you are and have. Study it, believe it, live in it, every day, every hour and every moment.

2. Just as it is the nature and glory of God to be always giving, it is the nature and glory of man to be always receiving. What did God make us for? Each of us have been made to be a vessel into which God can pour out His life, His beauty, His happiness and His love. We are created to be a receptacle and a reservoir of divine heavenly life and blessing, just as much as God can put into us. Have we understood this, that our great work -the object of our creation- is to be always receiving? If we fully enter into this, it will teach us some precious things. One thing -the utter folly of being proud or conceited should not be conceived. Suppose I were to borrow a very beautiful

dress, and walk about boasting of it as if it were my own, you might say, "What a fool!" Yet, here it is the Everlasting God that owns everything we have; shall we dare to exalt ourselves on account of what is all His?

We should be wise enough to appreciate what our position is with a God whose nature is to be always giving, and ours to be always receiving. Just as the lock and key fit each other, God the Giver and we the receiver fit into each other. How often we trouble about things, and about praying for them, instead of going back to the root of things, and saying, "Lord, I only crave to be the receptacle of what Your will is for me; of Your power and gifts and love and Your spirit." What can be more simple? Come as a receptacle; cleansed, emptied and humble. Come, and then God will delight to give you. I say it with all reverence that God cannot help Himself; it is His promise and His nature to give.

The blessing is ever flowing out of Him the same way water flows into the lowest places. If we could but be emptied and become nothing but receptacles, what a blessed life we would live! Day by day just praising Him; Thou give and I accept, Thou bestow and I rejoice to receive. How many tens of thousands of people have said this morning: "What a beautiful day! Let us throw open the windows and bring in the sunlight with its warmth and cheerfulness!" May our hearts learn every moment to drink in the light and sunshine of God's love. "Who am I, and what is my people, that we should be able to offer so willingly after this sort? For all things come of Thee, and we have given Thee of Thine own."

3. If God gives all and I receive all, then the third thought is very simple; I must give all back again. What a privilege that for the sake of having me in a loving, grateful relationship with Him, and giving me the happiness of pleasing and serving Him, the Everlasting God should say, "Come now, and bring Me back all that I gave." Yet people ask, "Oh, but must I give

everything back?" Brother, don't you know that there is no happiness or blessedness except in giving to God! David felt it. He said: "Lord, what an unspeakable privilege it is to be allowed to give that back to Thee which is Thine own!" Just to receive and then to render back in love to Him as God, what He gives.

Do you know what God needs you for? People say, "Does not God give us all good gifts to enjoy?" But do you know that the reality of the enjoyment is in the giving back? Just look at Jesus; God gave Him a wonderful body. He kept it holy and gave it as a sacrifice to God. This is the beauty of having a body. God has given you a soul; this is the beauty of having a soul, you can give it back to God. People talk about the difficulty they meet with in having so strong a will. You never can have too strong a will, but the trouble is we do not give that strong will up to God, to make it a vessel in which God can and will pour His Spirit, so as to fit it to do splendid service for Himself.

We have now had the three thoughts: God gives all; I receive all; I give up all. Will you do this now? Will not every heart say, "My God, teach me to give up everything?" Take your head, your mind with all its power of speaking, your property, your heart with its affections-the best and most secret -take gold and silver, everything, and lay it at God's feet and say, "Lord, here is the covenant between me and Thee. Thou delights to give all, and I delight to give back all." God teach us that. If that simple lesson were learnt, there would be an end to so much trouble about finding out the will of God, and an end to all our holding back, for it would be written, not upon our foreheads, but across our hearts, "God can do with me what He pleases; I belong to Him with all I have." Instead of always saying to God, "Give, give, give," we should say, "Yes, Lord, Thou dost give, thou dost love to give, and I love to give back." Try that life and find out if it is not the very highest life.

4. God gives all, I receive all, I give all. Now comes the fourth thought: God does so rejoice in what we give to Him. We are not the only ones who receive and the give, but God is a Giver and Receiver too. Once again, I say with reverence that God has more pleasure in the receiving back than even in giving. With our little faith we often think they come back to God again all defiled. God says, "No, they come back beautiful and glorified." The surrender of the dear child of His, with his aspirations and thanksgivings, brings it to God with a new value and beauty. Ah! child of God you do not know how precious the gift that you bring to your Father, is in His sight. Have I not seen a mother give a chunk of cake, and the child comes and offers her a piece to share it with her? How she values the gift! And your God, oh, my friends, your God, His heart, His Father's heart of love longs to have you give Him everything.

It is a demand, but it is not a demand of a hard Master; it is the call of a loving Father, who knows that every gift you bring to Him will bind you closer to Himself, and every surrender you make will open your heart wider to get more of His spiritual gifts. Oh, friends! A gift to God has infinite value in His sight. It delights Him. He sees of the travail of His soul and is satisfied. And it brings unspeakable blessings to you.

These are the thoughts our text suggests; now comes the practical application. What is the lesson? We have learnt what the true dispositions of the Christian life are; to be and abide in continual dependence upon God. Become nothing, begin to understand that you are nothing but an earthen vessel into which God will shine down the treasure of His love. Blessed is the man who knows what it is to be nothing, to be just an empty vessel meet for God's use. Work, the Apostle says, for it is God who works in you to will and to do. Brethren, take the place of deep dependence on God. And then take the place of child-like trust and expectancy. Count upon your God to do for you everything that you can desire of Him. Honour God as a God who gives liberally. Honour God and believe that He asks nothing from you, but what He has already given. And then praise, surrender and consecrate yourself to him. Praise Him for it! Let every sacrifice to Him be a thank-offering. What are we going to consecrate? First of all our lives. There are perhaps men and women -young men and women- whose hearts are asking, "What do you want me to do, or do I become a missionary?" No, indeed, I do not ask you to do this. Deal with God, and come to Him and say, "Lord of all, I belong to Thee, I am absolutely at Thy disposal." Yield up yourselves.

There may be many who cannot go as Missionaries, but you can give up yourself to God to be consecrated to the work of His Kingdom. Let us bow down before Him. Let us give Him all our powers; our head to think for His Kingdom, our heart to go out in love for men, and however feeble you may be, come and say, "Lord, here I am, to live and die for Thy Kingdom." Some talk and pray about the filling of the Holy Spirit; let them pray more and believe more. But remember the Holy Spirit came to fill and equip men to be messengers of the Kingdom. You cannot expect to be filled with the Spirit unless you want to live for Christ's Kingdom. You cannot expect all the love, peace and joy of heaven to come into your life and be your treasure, unless you give them up absolutely to the Kingdom of God and possess and use them only for Him. It is the soul that is utterly given up to God that will receive in its emptying the fullness of the Holy Spirit.

Dear friends, we must consecrate not only ourselves -body and soul- but all that we have. Some of you may have children; perhaps you have an only child, and you dread the very idea of letting her/him go. Take care, God deserves your confidence, your love, and your surrender. I plead with you; take your children and say to Jesus: "Anything Lord, that pleases Thee." Educate your children for Jesus. God will help you to do it. He may not accept all of them, but He will accept of the will, and there will be a rich blessing in your soul for it.

Then there is money. When I hear appeals for money from every society; when I hear calculations as to what the Christians of England are spending on pleasure and the small amount given for Missions, I say there is something terrible in it. God's children with so much wealth and comfort, giving away so small a portion. God be praised for every exception! But there are many who give but very little and those who never give so that it costs them something, and they feel it. Oh, friends, our giving must be in proportion to God's giving. He gives you all. Let us take it up in our consecration prayer: "Lord, take it all, every penny I possess. It is all Thine." Let us often say "It is all His." You may not know how much you ought to give. Give up all, put everything in His hands, and He will teach you if you will wait.

We have heard this precious message from David's mouth. We Christians of the 21st century, have we learnt to know our God who is willing to give everything? God will help us to. And then the second message. We have nothing that we do not receive, and we may receive everything if we are willing to stand before God and take it.

Thirdly. Whatever you have received from God give it back. It brings double blessings to your own soul. Fourthly. Whatever God receives back from us comes to Him in Heaven and gives Him infinite joy and happiness, as He sees His objective has been achieved. Let us come in the spirit of David, with the spirit of Jesus Christ in us. Let us pray our consecration prayer. And may the blessed spirit give each of us grace to think and to say the right thing, and to do what shall be pleasing in the Father's sight.

Dare Osatimehin

10

THE SOURCE AND STRENGTH OF THE TRIUMPHANT LIFE

Daniel 1:8
Freedom is not the right to do as you please, but the liberty to do as you ought

Daniel lived a triumphant life in Babylon. He lived a clean life in an unclean society, a holy life in an unholy society, a pure life in an impure nation, a righteous life in an idolatrous environment, and an undefiled life in the midst of moral defilement. He was like a white lily growing in a dirty environment without any stain on it. The source of his triumphant life was divine and the strength of that life was prayer and faith. The root of his principled life was God's grace and the sustaining power was his firm decision, importunate prayer life and unwavering faith in God.

With his spirit focused on God's glory and his heart given to God from which He could rule and reign without a rival, his firm purpose to remain faithful to God was absolute. Believers in Babylon must take heed to watch and pray lest they partake in the sins and lifestyle of Babylon. The culture of Babylon must not be allowed to defile the conscience of believers.

Daniel had no choice whether to live in Babylon or not; he had been taken captive along with other Jews from Jerusalem in Judah. But he had a choice as to what kind of life he lived. He chose to live a life free from every form of defilement. Defilement was not limited to eating and drinking either in the Old Testament or in the New Testament but he purposed in his heart that he would not defile himself. Unclean meat, food or meat sacrificed to idols, idolatry, witchcraft and sorcery, immorality, transgression and sin, evil of every kind all defile the man (Lev. 11:44,45; 18:24,30; 19:31; Ezekiel 20:7,18,19,43; 37:23; 1 Chron. 5:1; Hebrews 13:4; Psalm 106:39-42; Matt. 15:18-20).

Lev. 11:44 - For I am Jehovah your God; and ye shall hallow yourselves, and ye shall be holy; for I am holy; and ye shall not make yourselves unclean through any manner of crawling thing which creepeth on the earth
Lev 11:45 - For I am Jehovah who brought you up out of the land of Egypt, to be your God: ye shall therefore be holy, for I am holy
Lev. 18:24 - Make not yourselves unclean in any of these things; for in all these have the nations which I am casting out before you made themselves unclean
Lev.18:30 - And ye shall observe my charge that ye commit not any of the abominable customs which were committed before you; and ye shall not make yourselves unclean therein: I am Jehovah your God
Lev. 19:31 --Turn not unto necromancers and unto soothsayers; seek not after them to make yourselves unclean: I am Jehovah your God.

Matt. 15:18 - but the things which go forth out of the mouth come out of the heart and those defile man
Matt. 15:19 - For out of the heart come forth evil thoughts, murders, adulteries, fornications, thefts, false witnessings, blasphemies
Matt. 15:20 - These are the things which defile man; but the eating with unwashen hands does not defile man.

Ezekiel 20:7 - And I said unto them, Cast ye away every man the abominations of his eyes, and defile not yourselves with the idols of Egypt: I am Jehovah your God

Ezekiel 20:18- And I said unto their children in the wilderness,

Walk not in the statutes of your fathers, neither keep their ordinances, nor defile yourselves with their idols
Ezekiel 20:19 - I am Jehovah your God: walk in my statutes, and keep mine ordinances, and do them
Ezekiel 20:20 - And hallow my Sabbaths; and they shall be a sign between me and you, that ye may know that I am Jehovah your God

Psalm 106:39 - And they were defiled with their works, and went a-whoring in their doings.
Psalm 106:40 - Then was the anger of Jehovah kindled against his people, and he abhorred his inheritance;
Psalm 106:41 - And he gave them into the hand of the nations; and they that hated them ruled over them:
Psalm 106:42 - And their enemies oppressed them, and they were brought into subjection under their hand.

Daniel knew that defilement would bring God's judgment and wrath on him, so he purposed in his heart that he would not defile himself. Like Daniel, we too can have God's grace and spiritual strength to be free from all defilement of idolatry, alcoholism immorality and iniquity.

1. Consecration and purpose of heart against defilement

Daniel 1:8, Psalm 17:3, Deut. 32:46,47, Joshua 22:5; Psalms119:105,106; 119:1-3; 141:4; Prov. 4:23-27; Luke 9:51; Col. 3:1,2; 2 Tim. 3:10-14; Acts 11:23.

"But Daniel purposed in his heart." Out of the heart are the issues of life. Daniel's heart had been enlightened by the Word of God. A strong conviction had been established in his heart and to him truth was not relative but absolute. He judged the proposal and provision of the king by the demand of God, the great King of heaven and earth. He meditated much on the Word of God and considered the danger and eternal consequence of defiling himself. Regardless of the consequences of rejecting Babylon's lifestyle he purposed in his heart to fear God rather than men - even men of authority and might. His purpose was to please God and leave the consequences in His Hands. Fear of man destroys faith in God, faithfulness to God and the very foundation of a righteous life. Fear of man weakens the heart, enfeebles convictions and shakes the very foundation of a firm purpose.

Deut 32:45 - And when Moses had ended speaking all these words to all Israel
Deut 32:46 - He said unto them, set your hearts unto all the words that I testify among you this day, which ye shall command your children to take heed to do, all the words of this law
Deut 32:47 - For it is no vain word for you, but it is your life, and through this word ye shall prolong your days on the land whereunto ye pass over the Jordan to possess it

Psalm 119:105 - Thy word is a lamp unto my feet, and a light unto my path
Psalm 119:106 - I have sworn, and I will perform it, that I will keep thy righteous judgments
Psalm 119:1 - Blessed are the perfect in the way, who walk in the law of Jehovah
Psalm 119:2 - Blessed are they that observe his testimonies, that seek him with the whole heart
Psalm 119:3 - Who also do no unrighteousness: they walk in his ways

2 Tim. 3:10 - But thou hast been thoroughly acquainted with my teaching, conduct, purpose, faith, longsuffering, love, endurance
2 Tim. 3:11- Persecutions, sufferings: what sufferings happened to me in Antioch, in Iconium, in Lystra; what persecutions I endured; and the Lord delivered me out of all.
2 Tim. 3:12 - And all indeed who desire to live piously in Christ Jesus will be persecuted

2 Tim. 3:13- But wicked men and juggling impostors shall advance in evil, leading and being led astray

2 Tim. 3:14 -But thou, abide in those things which thou hast learned, and of which thou hast been fully persuaded, knowing of whom thou hast learned them

2 Tim. 3:15 - And that from a child thou hast known the sacred letters, which are able to make thee wise unto salvation, through faith which is in Christ Jesus

2 Tim. 3:16 - Every scripture is divinely inspired, and profitable for teaching, for conviction, for correction, for instruction in righteousness

2 Tim. 3:17 - That the man of God may be complete, fully fitted to every good work

Col. 3:1 - If therefore ye have been raised with the Christ, seek the things which are above, where the Christ is, sitting at the right hand of God

Col. 3:2 - Have your mind on the things that are above, not on the things that are on the earth

Col. 3:3 - For ye have died, and your life is hid with the Christ in God

Daniel purposed in his heart' not in his head. The heart, not the head, is the seat of our spiritual life, the spring of life's principles, the source of strong affection and man's actions, the fountain from which all spiritual and vital actions flow. As the heart is, so our life will be. Our lives can never rise above the state of our hearts. A conviction that originates from a sanctified heart, a principle that is rooted in a purified heart, a purpose that is implanted in a renewed heart, will lead to a righteous and holy life. Convictions floating like unsettled notions in the mind, borrowed principles stored in the head, shared by friends but not fixed and rooted in the heart do not produce sanctified or triumphant lives. When the heart is quickened and sanctified by God's grace, the life of faith and holiness will be a constant reality wherever we find ourselves - in Jerusalem or in Babylon. A firm, settled purpose of heart is indispensable for a consistently righteous life in Christ.

2. Comprehension and perception of a heart free from defilement

Daniel 1:8, Acts 15:22-29, Mark 7:20-23, Hebrews 12:15-17, James 3:6, Matt. 15:10-11,18-20, Psalm 119:1-3, James 1:26-27, Hebrews 13:4; Rev. 21:27.

In preserving himself holy and acceptable to God while training in the Babylonian school and living in the world's pagan city, Daniel's purpose of heart was to keep himself pure and free from all defilement. Daniel's definition and understanding of 'things that defile' was based on the scriptures he had been taught from childhood. For the Israelites, unclean animals and birds, meat sacrificed to idols and wine, part of which had been poured as libation to an idol, were all defiled and defiling. These provisions from the king's table were thus defiled and Daniel's conscience would not accept such free provisions.

So, he purposed in his heart that he would not defile himself with the portion of the king's meat, nor with the wine which he drank. This is a divine truth and lesson for all families and our Sunday school teachers and those that have contact with youths and children of today; that nothing can and should replace the foundational teaching of the bible principles of life. Our heritage and that of our children will depend on what we teach them when they are young, so that when they grow up, they will not depart from it. Solid foundation in the word of God is not negotiable, it is a choice that must be done and a duty that we owe this generation.

Acts 15:22 - Then it seemed good to the apostles and to the elders, with the whole assembly, to send chosen men from among them with Paul and Barnabas to Antioch, Judas called Barsabas and Silas, leading men among the brethren

Acts 15:23 - Having by their hand written thus: The apostles, and the elders, and the brethren, to the brethren who are from among the nations at Antioch, and in Syria and Cilicia, greeting
Acts15:24 - Inasmuch as we have heard that some who went out from amongst us have troubled you by words, upsetting your souls, saying that ye must be circumcised and keep the law ; to whom we gave no commandment
Acts 15:25 - It seemed good to us, having arrived at a common judgment, to send chosen men to you with our beloved Barnabas and Paul
Acts 15:26 - Men who have given up their lives for the name of our Lord Jesus Christ
Acts 15:27 - We have therefore sent Judas and Silas, who themselves also will tell you by word of mouth the same things
Acts 15:28 - For it has seemed good to the Holy Spirit and to us to lay upon you no greater burden than these necessary things
Acts 15:29 - To abstain from things sacrificed to idols, and from blood, and from what is strangled, and from fornication; keeping yourselves from which ye will do well. Farewell.

Hebrews 12:14 - Pursue peace with all, and holiness, without which no one shall see the Lord
Hebrews 12:15 - Watching lest there be any one who lacks the grace of God; lest any root of bitterness springing up trouble you , and many be defiled by it
Hebrews 12:16 - Lest there be any fornicator, or profane person, as Esau, who for one meal sold his birth right
Hebrews 12:17 - For ye know that also afterwards, desiring to inherit the blessing, he was rejected, (for he found no place for repentance) although he sought it earnestly with tears.

That which defileth man goes beyond idolatrous food and drink. Daniel knew this and we ought to know it as well, so that we can be cleansed and remain free from all filthiness (defilement) of the flesh and spirit, perfecting holiness in the fear of God (2 Cor. 7:1). To keep himself unspotted from the world and undefiled in the way (James 1:27; Psalm 119:1), the believer must be free from the abominable customs of the world (Lev. 8:30; 1 Peter 4:3,4), from any involvement with familiar spirits, wizards (Lev. 19:31), from all evil and transgressions (Ezekiel 20:43; 37:23); we must be watchful over ourselves so that we are not defiled with our own works or our own inventions (Psalm 106:39,40). The teaching of Christ ought to be taken to heart as we purpose in our hearts not to be defiled.

"And he said, That which cometh out of the man, that defileth the man. For from within, out of the heart of men, proceed evil thoughts, adulteries, fornications, murders, Thefts, covetousness, wickedness, deceit, lasciviousness, an evil eye, blasphemy, pride, foolishness: All these evil things come from within, and defile the man," (Mark 7:20-23). The Son of God can make us free and keep us free from all defilement - from all sin. His power can make you what you ought to be, His Blood can cleanse your heart and make you free; His love can fill your soul and make you live a victorious and triumphant life.

3. Clear conscience and purity of heart without defilement

Daniel 1:8; Acts 24:16; Hebrews 13:18; 1 Peter 3:15, 16; 1 Tim. 1:5, 19; Psalm 24:3, 4; Matt. 5:8; Acts 15:9; 2 Tim. 2:21, 22; Eph. 5:25-27.

"But Daniel purposed in his heart that he would not defile himself ... therefore he requested of the prince of the eunuchs that he might not defile himself." Daniel's aim in all things, in all places, in all situations, circumstances and at all times, was to have a conscience void of offence toward God. His was a noble pattern of life based on a noble principle of conviction. Whatever the cost or consequence, God's glory was the focus of his life. His great and noble desire was to be pure, to be free from every form of defilement, to please the Lord, and no pain, peril or possible persecution could bend his will to Babylon's culture or religious practice. His constant aim was to do whatever God demanded and to avoid whatever God forbade. He had been well-taught in the Scripture of truth, his spirit was responsive to God's still, small voice, his heart was pure and holy, his motive was God-honouring and self-effacing, and his conscience was enlightened and sensitive. Not even an appearance of evil would he excuse or allow in his life.

His private life was to be as pure as his public life. Even in Babylon, Daniel refused to allow anything defiling into his mind, his spirit, his heart, his body, his life, anything which would offend God, anything contrary to God's truth, purity or His pure worship and excellence. Oh, that we might live such a Christ-honouring life today. Oh, that we can have many Daniels that will be willing to be a friend of God first in our world of today.

Acts 24:16 - For this cause I also exercise myself to have in everything a conscience without offence towards God and men.
Hebrews 13:18 - Pray for us: for we persuade ourselves that we have a good conscience, in all things desirous to walk rightly.

1 Peter 3:15 - But sanctify the Lord the Christ in your hearts, and be always prepared to give an answer to everyone that asks you to give an account of the hope that is in you, but with meekness and fear
1 Peter 3:16 - Having a good conscience, that as to that in which they speak against you as evildoers, they may be ashamed who calumniate your good conversation in Christ.

Eph. 5:25 - Husbands, love your own wives, even as the Christ also loved the assembly, and has delivered himself up for it
Eph. 5:26 - In order that he might sanctify it, purifying it by the washing of water by the word
Eph. 5:27 - That he might present the assembly to himself

glorious, having no spot, or wrinkle, or any of such things; but that it might be holy and blameless

2 Tim. 2:21 - If therefore one shall have purified himself from these, in separating himself from them, he shall be a vessel to honour, sanctified, serviceable to the Master, prepared for every good work.
2 Tim. 2:22 - But youthful lusts flee, and pursue righteousness, faith, love, peace, with those that call upon the Lord out of a pure heart.

Dare to be a Daniel, dare to stand alone. Dare to stand firm for a purpose. Dare to make it known. Many mighty men are lost, daring not to stand. Dare to be a Daniel. Have a firm purpose to stand for truth and righteousness; be faithful in small things as well as in great things. Purpose in your heart to be undefiled and pray for grace to live as God commands. It is possible, you can do it, you will do it. God does not help those who will not act for every act of faith must be followed by an activity of faith. Put activity in your acts of faith, and God will stand by you. He has promised that he will not leave us alone or forsake us. Stand on His word, believe in His promises. If Daniel could do it, I am certain that you can do it too.

11

LIVING TO PLEASE THE LORD

Gal. 1:10; Romans 8:5-8; Matt. 17:5; 1 John 2:6
Live as if Christ died yesterday, arose this morning,
and is coming back tomorrow

Christ the beloved Son of God came to raise up sons unto God. He lived to please the Father and He has saved us so that we too can please Him in all things and at all times. When we are genuinely born again, there will be that desire in our hearts to want to please the Lord and to want to live in a way that His name will be glorified. We find in the lives of many people that were born again such as Paul the apostle, the desire and determination to please the Lord at all times and in all things. It takes the new birth or genuine conversion to please the Lord. Except we are born again, we cannot please the Lord. When Jesus was on the earth, He pleased God and this is what God wants from everyone – to please Him. Actually, He wants every one of us to live like the Lord Jesus Christ of Whom He testified: "This is my beloved Son, in whom I am well pleased; hear ye him."

The lack of desire, decision and determination to please God with your character, dressing and in all things, at all times is evidence of a carnal nature and proof of insensitivity to the Spirit of God.

When someone is born again pleasing the Lord will be:
- Priority of his life; the most important thing in his life
- His purpose for living; in any situation, condition, place and community he finds himself, his purpose for

living will be to please the Lord
- His pursuit in learning; the reason why he studies the bible, attends Christian fellowships and listens to sermons
- Proof of his love to the Lord
- Pattern of his lifestyle
- His principle in labour; he does not work just to receive salary
- Parameter and perimeter for his liberty; like Christ, the liberty he enjoys is always guided by his decision and determination to please the Lord.

1. Sinful lifestyles that provoke the Lord

Romans 1:28-32; Jer. 32:30-33; Ezekiel 8:17,18; Psalm 106:29; 73:6-11; 109:18,19; Isaiah 3:8-24; Zeph. 1:8,9; Deut. 22:5.

To please the Lord, we must know those things that displease Him; we must know the kind of character, conduct and behaviour that provoke the Lord. We must not be like the children of Israel who purportedly returned, only to provoke the Lord to anger with their evil deeds. On the contrary, the Lord expects a returning backslider to have a change of life, a change of disposition and a change of behaviour.

We provoke the Lord when we not only behave like the Egyptians (the world), but also seem to add a new angle to their evil and corrupt lifestyles. Sinful actions do displease and provoke the Lord. Salvation leads us to love the Lord and to avoid any act that can provoke Him. The abomination of the world, sinful practices and immodest style of dressing provoke Him to anger and to judgment. There are some people that copy the pattern and style of their dressing from newspaper and magazine models, so called celebrities, musicians and politicians. But a real child of God bases his or her style of dressing on the prescriptions of the Scriptures, on 'thus saith the Lord.' The Christian pattern of dressing should not be copied from newspapers, magazine or catalogue books of the world but from the principles of the word of God. The world comes into the church because the church copies from the world. The church is in conformity with the world instead of being transformed by the renewing of our minds. We try to copy the world instead of the world copying the church. Dressing in strange apparels means dressing in apparels that do not fulfil the purpose of God for creating dress materials. There is no reason to disobey God. What He hated in the Old Testament, He still hates in the New Testament.

Romans 1:28 - And according as they did not think good to have God in their knowledge, God gave them up to a reprobate mind to practice unseemly things
Romans 1:29 - Being filled with all unrighteousness, wickedness, covetousness, malice; full of envy, murder, strife, deceit, evil dispositions; whisperers
Romans 1:30 - Back-biters, hateful to God, insolent, proud, boasters, inventors of evil things, disobedient to parents
Romans 1:31 - Void of understanding, faithless, without natural affection, unmerciful
Romans 1:32 - Who knowing the righteous judgment of God, that they who do such things are worthy of death, not only practice them, but have fellow delight in those who do them.

Jer. 32:30 - For the children of Israel and the children of Judah have been doing only evil in my sight from their youth; for the children of Israel have only provoked me to anger with the work of their hands, saith Jehovah
Jer. 32:31 - For this city hath been to me a provocation of mine anger and of my fury from the day that they built it even unto this day; that I should remove it from before my face
Jer. 32:32 - Because of all the evil of the children of Israel and of the children of Judah, which they have done to provoke me to anger, they, their kings, their princes, their priests, and their prophets, and the men of Judah, and the inhabitants of

Jerusalem
Jer. 32:33 - And they have turned unto me the back, and not the face; and though I taught them, rising early and teaching, they hearkened not to receive instruction.

Psalm 73:6 - Therefore pride encompasseth them as a neck-chain; violence covereth them as a garment
Psalm 73:7 - Their eyes stand out from fatness, they exceed the imaginations of their heart
Psalm 73:8 - They mock and speak wickedly of oppression, they speak loftily
Psalm 73:9 - They set their mouth in the heavens, and their tongue walketh through the earth
Psalm 73:10 - Therefore his people turn hither and waters in fullness are wrung out to them
Psalm 73:11 - And they say, How can *God know, and is there knowledge in the Most High?

Isaiah 3:8 - For Jerusalem stumbleth and Judah falleth, because their tongue and their doings are against Jehovah, to provoke the eyes of his glory
Isaiah 3:9 - The look of their face doth witness against them, and they declare their sin as Sodom: they hide it not. Woe unto their soul! for they have brought evil upon themselves
Isaiah 3:10 - Say ye of the righteous that it shall be well with him, for they shall eat the fruit of their doing.
Isaiah 3:11 - Woe unto the wicked! it shall be ill with him, because the desert of his hands shall be rendered unto him
Isaiah 3:12 - As for my people, children are their oppressors, and women rule over them. My people! they that guide thee mislead thee, and destroy the way of thy paths
Isaiah 3:13 - Jehovah setteth himself to plead, and standeth to judge the peoples
Isaiah 3:14 - Jehovah will enter into judgment with the elders of his people and their princes, saying: It is ye that have eaten up the vineyard: the spoil of the poor is in your houses
Isaiah 3:15 - What mean ye that ye crush my people, and grind

the faces of the afflicted? saith the Lord, Jehovah of hosts
Isaiah 3:16 - And Jehovah said, Because the daughters of Zion are haughty, and walk with stretched-out neck and wanton eyes, and go along mincing, and making a tinkling with their feet
Isaiah 3:17 - Therefore the Lord will make bald the crown of the head of the daughters of Zion, and Jehovah will lay bare their secret parts
Isaiah 3:18 - In that day the Lord will take away the ornament of anklets, and the little suns and crescents
Isaiah 3:19 - The pearl-drops, and the bracelets, and the veils
Isaiah 3:20 - The head-dresses, and the stepping chains, and the girdles, and the scent-boxes, and the amulets
Isaiah 3:21 - The finger-rings, and the nose-rings
Isaiah 3:22 - The festival-robes, and the tunics, and the mantles, and the wallets
Isaiah 3:23 - The mirrors, and the fine linen bodices, and the turbans, and the flowing veils
Isaiah 3:24 - And it shall come to pass, instead of perfume there shall be rottenness; and instead of a girdle, a rope; and instead of well-set hair, baldness; and instead of a robe of display, a girding of sackcloth; brand instead of beauty
Isaiah 3:25 - Thy men shall fall by the sword, and thy mighty in the fight
Isaiah 3:26 - And her gates shall lament and mourn; and, stripped, she shall sit upon the ground.

2. Scriptural lifestyles that please the Lord

2 Tim. 2:4; 1 Thess. 4:1; Romans 12:1,2; 15:3; John 8:29; 1 John 2:15-17; 1 Tim. 2:8

We do not entangle ourselves with the beliefs and practices of the world because we want to please God. True Christians should not conform to the dress patterns, burial ceremonies and lifestyles of the world; if we are true followers of Christ, we will not please ourselves but always seek to do those things that please our heavenly Father . Even Christ did not seek to please himself. To please the Father, we must do the will of God in all things and at all times.

The life that pleases God is one built on Scriptural principles. These should guide us in all things and at all times. These principles apply to our character, behaviour, our morals and to everything that we do, especially our dressing. There are some principles that need to guide our style of dressing.

These are:
- The purpose of our dressing – it must be to cover our nakedness properly, neatly and appropriately – Rev. 2:16.
- The precaution in our dressing – we should dress in such a way as to avoid being classified with the wrong kind of people as was the case with Judah's daughter-in-law and Moses, on account of their attires – Gen. 38:20-22; Exodus 2:16-19.
- The preservation of souls and moral values in our dressing – it must be with the aim of not constituting an object of temptation to other souls – Romans 12:1, 2.
- The precept concerning our dressing – it must be with the aim of keeping to God's word which remains the same at all times and in all ages – Deut. 22:5; 1 Tim. 2:9.
- The practice in dressing – it must be with the aim of letting moderation rule our sense of dressing; we are neither archaic nor too modernistic – Luke 21:34; Phil. 4:5.
- The purity through our dressing – the purpose of our dressing should be to promote purity and make for a rapture-able life, rather than mere adornment – 1 Peter 3:3, 4.

- The priority – the ultimate goal of our life should be to please the Lord so that any time He comes, we will be able to go with Him – Isaiah 43:7,21; Hebrews 12:14; 11:5.

Romans 12:1 - I beseech you therefore, brethren, by the compassions of God, to present your bodies a living sacrifice, holy, acceptable to God, which is your intelligent service
Romans12:2 - And be not conformed to this world, but be transformed by the renewing of your mind, that ye may prove what is the good and acceptable and perfect will of God.

1John 2:15 - Love not the world, nor the things in the world. If anyone loves the world, the love of the Father is not in him;
1John 2:16 - Because all that is in the world, the lust of the flesh, and the lust of the eyes, and the pride of life, is not of the Father, but is of the world.
1John 2:17 - And the world is passing, and its lust, but he that does the will of God abides for eternity.

1Tim. 2:8 I will therefore that the men pray in every place, lifting up pious hands, without wrath or reasoning.

3. Sober lifestyles proclaimed by the Lord

Luke 21:34-36; Mark 4:18,19,23-25; Luke 12:34-48; Titus 2:2,4,6,12; 1 Tim. 2:9,15; 1 Peter 5:5-8; 1 Thess. 5:6; 1 Peter 4:7,15-18

The kind of life that the Lord advocates is a sober lifestyle at all times - times of wedding, funeral, naming ceremony, church service, office hours or school times. The Lord wants us to live a sober life, a life that He approves of and one that pleases Him. There will be punishment for the people that know the Word of God but don't obey.

Luke 12:34 - For where your treasure is, there also will your heart be

Luke 12:35 - Let your loins be girded about, and lamps burning

Luke 12:36 - And ye like men who wait their own lord whenever he may leave the wedding, that when he comes and knocks, they
may open to him immediately

Luke 12:37 - Blessed are those bondmen whom the lord on coming shall find watching; verily I say unto you, that he will gird himself
and make them recline at table, and coming up will serve them

Luke 12:38 - And if he come in the second watch, and come in the third watch, and find them thus, blessed are those bondmen

Luke 12:39 - But this know, that if the master of the house had known in what hour the thief was coming, he would have watched,
and not have suffered his house to be dug through

Luke 12:40 - And ye therefore, be ye ready, for in the hour in which ye do not think it, the Son of man comes

Luke 12:41 - And Peter said to him, Lord, sayest thou this parable to us, or also to all?

Luke 12:42 - And the Lord said, Who then is the faithful and prudent steward, whom his lord will set over his household, to give the measure of corn in season?

Luke 12:43 - Blessed is that bondman whom his lord on coming shall find doing thus

Luke 12:44 - Verily I say unto you, that he will set him over all that he has

Luke 12:45 - But if that bondman should say in his heart, My lord delays to come, and begin to beat the menservants and the maidservants, and to eat and to drink and to be drunken

Luke 12:46 - The lord of that bondman shall come in a day when he does not expect it, and in an hour he knows not of, and shall cut
him in two and appoint his portion with the unbelievers

Luke 12:47 - But that bondman who knew his own lord's will,

and had not prepared himself nor done his will, shall be beaten with many stripes
Luke 12:48 - But he who knew it not, and did things worthy of stripes, shall be beaten with few. And to everyone to whom much has been given, much shall be required from him; and to whom men have committed much, they will ask from him the more

1Peter 5:5 - Likewise ye younger, be subject to the elder, and all of you bind on humility towards one another; for God sets himself against the proud, but to the humble gives grace
1Peter 5:6 - Humble yourselves therefore under the mighty hand of God, that he may exalt you in the due time
1Peter 5:7 - Having cast all your care upon him, for he cares about you
1Peter 5:8 - Be vigilant, watch. Your adversary the devil as a roaring lion walks about seeking whom he may devour

The Lord calls us to a life of sobriety – the aged and the young. Our character and conduct should reflect sobriety, watchfulness, prayerfulness, obedience and faithfulness to the teachings of the Lord. We should not be careless, frivolous and deliberately disobedient to the Word of God. It is only as we live in accordance with His Word that we will have hope of being raptured at His coming.

1Peter 4:7 - But the end of all things is drawn nigh: be sober therefore, and be watchful unto prayers
1Peter 4:15 - Let none of you suffer indeed as murderer, or thief, or evildoer, or as overseer of other people's matters
1Peter 4:16 - But if as a Christian, let him not be ashamed, but glorify God in this name
1Peter 4:17 - For the time of having the judgment begin from the house of God is come ; but if first from us, what shall be the end of those who obey not the glad tidings of God?
1Peter 4:18 - And if the righteous is difficultly saved, where shall the impious and the sinner appear?

"The end of all things is at hand: be ye therefore sober, and watch unto prayer." The conviction that we have and the way we live may bring sufferings and persecution across our paths, but we are not to relent in our efforts.

12

THE SURRENDERED CONSECRATED LIFE

Nothing is ever dull when you are walking in the supernatural with God. If you must hammer; build something

Numbers 6:1 - And Jehovah spoke to Moses, saying
Numbers 6:2 - Speak unto the children of Israel, and say unto them, If a man or a woman have vowed the special vow of a Nazarite, to consecrate themselves to Jehovah
Numbers 6:3 - He shall separate himself from wine and strong drink: he shall drink no vinegar of wine, nor vinegar of strong drink, neither shall he drink any liquor of grapes, nor eat grapes, fresh or dried
Numbers 6:4 - All the days of his separation shall he eat nothing that is made of the vine, from the seed-stones, even to the skin
Numbers 6:5 - All the days of the vow of his separation there shall no razor come upon his head; until the days be fulfilled, that he hath consecrated himself to Jehovah, he shall be holy; he shall let the locks of the hair of his head grow
Numbers 6:6 - All the days that he hath consecrated himself to Jehovah, he shall come near no dead body
Numbers 6:7 - He shall not make himself unclean for his father, or for his mother, for his brother, or for his sister when they die; for the consecration of his God is upon his head
Numbers 6:8 - All the days of his separation he is holy to Jehovah

Romans 12:1 - I beseech you therefore, brethren, by the

compassions of God, to present your bodies a living sacrifice, holy, acceptable to God, which is your intelligent service
Romans 12:2 - And be not conformed to this world, but be transformed by the renewing of your mind, that ye may prove what is the good and acceptable and perfect will of God
Col. 3:5 - Put to death therefore your members which are upon the earth, fornication, uncleanness, vile passions, evil lust, and unbridled desire, which is idolatry
Col. 3:6 - On account of which things the wrath of God comes upon the sons of disobedience
Col. 3:7 - In which ye also once walked when ye lived in these things
Col. 3:8 - But now, put off, ye also, all these things, wrath, anger, malice, blasphemy, vile language out of your mouth
Col. 3:9 - Do not lie to one another, having put off the old man with his deeds
Col. 3:10 - And having put on the new, renewed into full knowledge according to the image of him that has created him

The subject of consecration is central to the Christian life and walk. It determines to what extent a believer will go in his relationship and fellowship with God. Whether or not he would attain the status of a 'Friend of God' like Abraham or 'a man after my own heart' like David is predicated on the level of his consecration and surrender to the Lord. Abraham did not earn this title only because God loved him but equally because he demonstrated uncommon surrender and obedience through consecration. Moses had the privilege of leading Israel out of a bondage of 400 years, not because he was the most educated, but perhaps because he chose 'rather to suffer affliction with the people of God, than to enjoy the pleasures of sin for a season; esteeming the reproach of Christ greater riches than the treasures in Egypt' (Hebrews 11:25,26). Paul got revelations and visions, and reached the third heavens because of his relationship and devotion to God (Gen. 22:1-18; Phil. 3:7-15).

Many believers manage to tread the periphery of the ocean of God's grace, power and revelation, because they are unwilling to go the extra mile with Him. Yet, the purpose of our call is that we 'may be able to comprehend with all saints what is the breadth, and length, and depth, and height; And to know the love of Christ, which passeth knowledge, that ye might be filled with all the fullness of God' (Eph. 3:18, 19). Many believers scarcely know 'what the riches of the glory of his inheritance in the saints, And what is the exceeding greatness of his power to us-ward who believe, according to the working of his mighty power' (Eph. 1:18, 19).

Why are some believers not effective in their ministries?

Consecration lifts the believer from the realm of the ordinary to the sublime. It releases us from the spoils of pleasure and sets us apart for God's use and service. A believer who is set apart for God attains greater heights and deeper depths. Consecration begins as an act of separating from a common to a sacred use, or of devoting and dedicating a person or thing to the service and worship of God. Consecration does not necessarily make a person or a thing holy, but declares it to be set apart; that is, devoted to God or to divine service like the consecration of the priests among the Israelites and the consecration of the vessels used in the temple (Exodus 29:9; Lev. 8:12; Numbers 3:3; Joshua 6:19; Acts 6:6; 13:3).

CALL TO CONSECRATION AND TOTAL SURRENDER
(Romans 12:1; Col. 3:1-5; Exodus 32:29; Numbers 32:12; 2 Kings 23:3; 2 Chron. 15:15).

"I beseech you therefore, brethren, by the mercies of God, that ye present your bodies a living sacrifice, holy, acceptable unto God, which is your reasonable service" (Romans 12:1). Paul here calls the children of God to a supreme act of surrender, consecration and devotion to the Lord. This he does with the tenderness of a father and consciousness of a fellow heir. He admonishes, implores and pleads, rather than command believers, to yield wholly to the Lord. Paul's plea here is against the background of the foundational stones of teachings he had laid in the preceding chapters on the grace of God, propitiation for sin, justification by faith, possibility of reconciliation, the ministry of the Holy Spirit and the covenant of God with the children of Israel.

The thought of the Apostle here zeroes in on two things: one, the fact that we are called brethren implies that before dedication and consecration can be meaningful, the new birth must have occurred. Two, since we have received the mercies of God, the only logical consequence of our gratitude is that we will now give our bodies unto the Lord as a living sacrifice.

Who are those called to offer themselves as living sacrifices?

The Apostle opines that there are those who are cleansed, and had become children of God. It is this bracket of people who have come into a dynamic living relationship with Jesus that are called to offer themselves unto God as a living sacrifice, holy and acceptable unto Him. And this is God's demand on everyone who professes the new birth. Those that are dead to sins and trespasses and the rudiments of this world are called to set their affections on heavenly things (Col. 3:1-5).

When God called Abraham, He summoned him to a higher, more perfect walk (Gen. 17:1). To Solomon, He said, "if thou wilt walk in my ways, to keep my statutes and my commandments, as thy father David did walk, then I will lengthen thy days" (1 Kings 3:14). Again, He challenged Israel as a nation to separate from sin and idolatry saying, "For Moses had said, Consecrate yourselves today to the Lord... that he may bestow upon you a blessing this day," (Exodus 32:29).

God does not accept a half-hearted service nor does He demand any relationship that falls short of entire consecration. Those who must know and receive of His best must be willing to lay themselves on the altar of sacrifice.

Further examples abound of individuals and groups of people who entirely served the Lord and reaped the reward of obedience. Caleb and Joshua were singled out for special blessings because they went beyond the run-of-the mill devotion to carve a niche in God's heart. While thousands of their colleagues died in the wilderness Caleb the son of Jephunneh, the Kenezite, and Joshua the son of Nun (were spared), for they had wholly followed the LORD (Numbers 32:12). They determined to go the extra mile with God when others settled for the easy walk. In a like manner, the tribe of Judah (at different times) under Josiah and Asa, covenanted to serve the Lord with their whole heart all their life (2 Kings 23:3; 2 Chron. 15:15).

The highest example of consecration and absolute surrender is found in our Lord Jesus Christ who gave His all for the redemption of the world. Love drove Him from the bliss of heaven, the praises of angels and the fellowship of His Father, to tread the dusty roads of Jerusalem in search of the lost.

REASONS FOR THE BELIEVER'S CONSECRATION
(Romans 12:1; Neh. 9:19-21; Psalm 103:1-5; Micah 7:18; Eph. 2:4,5; Titus 3:5; Psalm 116:12; Philemon 8-10).

God's call to consecration is not without basis. He has been gracious to mankind. His love to us is without measure knowing that none of His creatures enjoy as much benevolence as man that is created in His own image. He causes His sun to rise on the just and unjust and sends His rain upon the grass to give us our meal. More importantly, the believer owes God a greater debt of gratitude, first, for His saving grace that delivered us from sin and power of darkness and translated us into the kingdom of His dear Son (Col. 1:13). Now we are called 'brethren' — people washed in the blood of Jesus, justified and adopted into His Kingdom. We were brought from the depth of sin to sit with Christ in the heavenly places and have been made heirs of the grace of God.

Second, we must be grateful to God for His manifold mercies. No one qualifies for the mercy of God based on his own merit; it is His free gift to us. His bowel yearns for the care and welfare of His creatures. The prophet captures it this way: "It is of the LORD's mercies that we are not consumed, because his compassions fail not," (Lam. 3:22). A personal voluntary presentation of the believer to the Lord as a sacrifice follows the manifold grace and blessing he has received from God. This is the response that articulates our gratitude for the showers of blessing God has poured upon us.

Even though Israel did a lot to provoke the Lord to anger both in the wilderness and in Canaan, God did not forsake them. "Yet thou in thy manifold mercies forsakes them not in the wilderness: the pillar of the cloud departed not from them by day, to lead them in the way; neither the pillar of fire by night, to shew them light, and the way wherein they should go," (Neh.. 9:19).

The manifold mercies of God guarantee the presence of God in our lives. Reconciliation, the breaking down of the wall of partition between us and God is by the mercies of God. The leading of the Spirit of God in the life and ministry of a believer is also a manifestation of the mercies of God (Romans 8:14). The psalmist also shows how God manifested His mercy towards Him (Psalm 103:1-5). In response, he asked: "What shall I render unto the Lord for all his benefits toward me?" (Psalm 116:12). With the psalmist then and all the redeemed of the Lord today, it is 'the multitude of thy tender mercies' that blot out our sins and gives us life more abundantly.

What can the believer render unto the Lord for all His benefits? Having enjoyed such mercies, Apostle Paul says affirmatively that the only reasonable service we can offer to the Lord is to present ourselves unto Him, a living sacrifice, holy and acceptable. This is the only acceptable sacrifice that could express our gratitude for the mercies the Lord made manifest in our life through salvation, sanctification, Holy Ghost baptism, healing, deliverance, provision, grace and the promise of heaven.

Another reason for presenting 'our bodies a living sacrifice' to God is hinged on the sacrifice of Jesus. Nothing equals the price He paid for us at Calvary. He suffered like no other to bear our grief and carry our sorrows. And the only logical gratitude from those He died to save is to sing with the hymn-writer - When I survey the wondrous Cross On which the Prince of glory died.

Finally, the benefit of total consecration compels us to throw our lives unreservedly to the Lord. When we do, we shall become vessels of honour reserved for the Master's use (2 Tim. 2:21). Second, God's secrets shall remain with us (Gen. 18:17).

THE REASONABLE SERVICE OF SURRENDERED BELIEVERS
(Romans 12:1; 2 Cor. 8:3-5; Prov. 23:26; Romans 6:12, 13, 19; 1 Cor. 6:13, 19, 20; 1 Peter 3:10; Psalm 24:3, 4).

"...that ye present your bodies a living sacrifice, holy, acceptable unto God, which is your reasonable service" (Romans 12:1).

To present is to yield and surrender, or give as offering. And what we are to present, surrender or give to God as offering here is our body. The heart is the most important of all the parts of our body. It is the first thing we give to God. God makes a special demand of it. "My son, give me thine heart, and let thine eyes observe my ways," (Prov. 23:26). When our hearts are given to the Lord, we are cleansed and purged. Without this, consecration will be worthless and unprofitable.

Also all members of the believer's body must be daily and continually presented to the Lord in a definite act of consecration. Members of our body include the eyes, ears, tongue, hands, feet, etc. We should not employ our eyes to gaze upon objects of temptation. Rather, we are to concentrate on things that sponsor and promote holiness in our thoughts and actions. "I made a covenant with mine eyes; why then should I think upon a maid?" (Job 31:1). Here, Job consecrated his eyes for the glory of God and the promotion of holiness in his life. Also, we should not use our mouths or lips to crack indecent jokes or give our ears to hearing something that can inflame our thoughts. If we consecrate the members of our body to the Lord, we will do things that please Him.

OUR HOLY AND EXALTED PRIESTHOOD
(Numbers 6:1-8; 1 Peter 2:5, 9; Phil. 2:17; Luke 9:23).

In the Old Testament, priests were commissioned to offer daily, continual sacrifices unto the Lord. Nobody was a priest who did not offer sacrifice to the Lord. These people were commanded to sanctify themselves by virtue of their hallowed service. They were to distinguish themselves from others and separate from every form of defilement because they were people that drew nigh to God in the performance of religious duties. And as long as they officiated in this capacity, they were required to be consecrated.

The Nazarites (Jews who professed extraordinary purity of life and devotion) of the old dispensation were expected to abstain from everything that defiled as long as the vow of separation was upon them (Numbers 6:1-8). Such were obliged to be more strict and with closer devotion to the Lord than others. They would rather be held in derision by others than break their vows to be separated from the Lord. In the same vein, all true members of the body of Christ today as priests are to individually on a daily, continual basis 'offer up spiritual sacrifices, acceptable to God by Jesus Chris' (1 Peter 2:5). We are not to bring animal sacrifice to the Lord any more but to present our bodies a living sacrifice. A sacrifice is something you dedicate to the Lord. A Christian therefore, hands his life to God unconditionally, unreservedly and wholeheartedly. He presents himself to God to do His will only. "Then said I, Lo, I come (in the volume of the book it is written of me,) to do thy will, O God" (Hebrews 10:7).

How can the members of a believer's body be engaged as sacrifice unto the Lord? Strictly, the sacrifice we offer to the Lord must include our time, talents, resources and endowments. For instance, Dorcas spent her time and resources making dresses and giving to the poor. It might even be our voice employed in singing and ministering. The feet might be presented to the Lord in going from one place to another witnessing for Christ. Paul the Apostle spoke of the sacrificial giving of the churches in Macedonia for the cause of the gospel. They dug into the very sustenance of life and almost gave their very blood. But before they did that, they first gave themselves unto the Lord. Our souls must first experience God's love and receive His mercy before we can present ourselves to the Lord. How can a Christian bear his cross daily?

Again as a sacrifice, the believer must daily bear his cross and deny self. The sacrifice of Christ led Him to bear the cross. When we patiently bear reproach, ridicule and persecution for Christ's sake today it is part of the sacrificial life. "And he said to them all, If any man will come after me, let him deny himself, and take up his cross daily, and follow me" (Luke 9:23).

THE CHRISTIAN'S NON-CONFORMITY TO THE WORLD
(Romans 12:2; Gal. 6:14; James 1:27; 4:4; 2 Cor. 6:14-18; 1 John 2:15).

What is the Christian's position in relation to the world?

Our service to God cannot be acceptable if we are still unequally yoked together with the world. The true believer is wholly given to God so that he will not be conformed to the spirit of this age. The spirit of the age manifests itself in pride, ego, sinful entertainment or sensual pleasure. The world pervades the society through worldly music, movies, fashion, inordinate ambition and ungodly pursuits. The believer is delivered from the present evil world never to be friendly with or conformed to it. "But God forbid that I should glory, save in the cross of our Lord Jesus Christ, by whom the world is crucified unto me, and I unto the world" (Gal. 6:14). We must of necessity keep ourselves unspotted from the world.

13

THE SPIRIT CONTROLLED LIFE

Romans 8:1 -13
Nothing is ever dull when you are walking in the supernatural with God

"And because ye are sons, God hath sent forth the Spirit of his Son into your hearts, crying Abba, Father," (Gal. 4:6).

Romans 8:1- [There is] therefore now no condemnation to them which are in Christ Jesus, who walk not after the flesh, but after the Spirit
Romans 8:2 - For the law of the Spirit of life in Christ Jesus hath made me free from the law of sin and death
Romans 8:3 - For what the law could not do, in that it was weak through the flesh, God sending his own Son in the likeness of sinful flesh, and for sin, condemned sin in the flesh
Romans 8:4 -That the righteousness of the law might be fulfilled in us, who walk not after the flesh, but after the Spirit
Romans 8:5 - For they that are after the flesh do mind the things of the flesh; but they that are after the Spirit the things of the Spirit
Romans 8:6 - For to be carnally minded [is] death; but to be spiritually minded [is] life and peace
Romans 8:7 -Because the carnal mind [is] enmity against God: for it is not subject to the law of God, neither indeed can be
Romans 8:8 - So then they that are in the flesh cannot please God
Romans 8:9 - But ye are not in the flesh, but in the Spirit, if so be that the Spirit of God dwells in you. Now if any man have not the Spirit of Christ, he is none of his

Romans 8:10 - And if Christ [be] in you, the body [is] dead because of sin; but the Spirit [is] life because of righteousness
Romans 8:11 - But if the Spirit of him that raised up Jesus from the dead dwell in you, he that raised up Christ from the dead shall also quicken your mortal bodies by his Spirit that dwelleth in you
Romans 8:12 - Therefore, brethren, we are debtors, not to the flesh, to live after the flesh
Romans 8:13 - For if ye live after the flesh, ye shall die: but if ye through the Spirit do mortify the deeds of the body, ye shall live.

Paul in this epistle has spoken very highly and gloriously concerning the Christian life. His discourse on the life of a believer comes to a climax in this chapter. Many people remain in the struggle, confusion, and unfulfilled desires of the seventh chapter of Romans. But Paul, the Apostle did not stop there. He looked ahead to a better, greater, and more glorious hope for the convicted and awakened sinner.

In this chapter, the Lord reveals the truth concerning the Holy Spirit to us – the position, the power, the centrality of the Holy Spirit as the strength of the Christian life. The mention of the Holy Spirit comes up in the first verse of the chapter and runs on till the last verse of the chapter, just as He operates from the beginning to the end of the Christian life.

NEW LIFE AND NEW WALK IN THE SPIRIT
(Romans 8:1-4; John 5:24; Acts 13:39

"There is therefore now no condemnation to them which are in Christ Jesus, who walk not after the flesh, but after the Spirit. For the law of the Spirit of life in Christ Jesus hath made me free from the law of sin and death" (Romans 8:1, 2).

The convicted and awakened sinner who emerges out of the

tyranny of sin in the seventh chapter takes on a new fresh air and begins to bask in the newness of life found in Christ Jesus. This new life offers the greatest of freedom and a new kind of liberty obtainable in no other place. It frees the oppressed who have been tied down from all forms of condemnation.

Condemnation is the common experience of all those who are not in Christ Jesus. Guilt of sin is a common universal experience of all sinners. The sinner is condemned from all sides:

- The truth of the word of God condemns error, falsehood, and the life of deception that the sinner lives.
- God condemns sin because He is of purer eyes than to behold iniquity and He cannot see sin without condemning it.
- The righteous life of the saints also condemns sinners and shows them the sinfulness of their evil ways.

All these - God, the truth of God's word and the saintly life of the Christian – combine to bring condemnation upon the sinner. Besides these, the sinner's conscience neighbours the evil of his own ways as satan daily accuses the sinner and paints his sins in the grimmest colour.

Peace, joy, and justification come through forgiveness in Christ. There is no peace without a relationship with Christ. It is when we come into a personal relationship with Christ that we can be saved and free from condemnation.

"He that believeth on him is not condemned: but he that believeth not is condemned already because he hath not believed in the name of the only begotten Son of God" (John 3:18).

It is the Lord who was crucified on Calvary for our justification that can remove the burden of sin. Faith in Christ frees from guilt and condemnation of sin. When we are freed from condemnation, liberty, and new life follows.

It is strange to hear some people teach and preach that Paul was not free from sin. This cannot be true because the writings of Paul under the inspiration of the Holy Spirit shows how 'holy, unblame-able....' he conducted himself before them that believed in Thessalonica. Paul the Apostle knew what it meant to be free and have liberty from the tyranny of sin. He declared, "For the law of the Spirit of life in Christ Jesus hath made me free from the law of sin and death" (Romans 8:2).

Significantly, he observed that his freedom was not by his power or ability but the Lord Jesus Christ. Jesus alone can set free. "And ye shall know the truth, and the truth shall make you free" (John 8:32). The truth launched the helpless, spent and frustrated sinner of the seventh chapter of Romans free when he came into the experience of the eighth chapter. The truth unties the sinner bound to the apron strings of the taskmaster, the devil. The sacrifice of the Lord Jesus Christ sets us free. "If the Son therefore shall make you free, ye shall be free indeed," (John 8:36). We can surely be free from sin. To assert otherwise is to limit the power of the Lord Jesus Christ. Paul had earlier pointed to the fact that the Jews were relying on the Mosaic Law as though deliverance from sin could come through the law. He had, therefore empathised that by the deeds of the law there shall no flesh be justified in his sight: for by the law is the knowledge of sin, (Romans 3:20). He then went back and substantiated the flaw he observed in the law

"For what the law could not do, in that it was weak through the flesh, God sending his own Son in the likeness of sinful flesh, and for sin, condemned sin in the flesh: That the righteousness of the law might be fulfilled in us, who walk not after flesh, but after the Spirit," (Romans 8:3, 4). Christ died so that the righteousness of the law might be fulfilled in us.

We must observe that there were a lot of things (virtues or obedience to the law) the Old Testament people could not attain. They could not attain to the full obedience of the law because the law was weak through the flesh. But we are in Christ, we are living after the Cross and the purpose is that the righteousness of the law might be fulfilled in us who walk not after the flesh, but after the Spirit. This new change comes through Christianity. The ministration of the law could not have removed guilt and condemnation completely. The Christian life, once obtained, gives victory over the flesh (Romans 8:1, 9, 12).

"But put ye on the Lord Jesus Christ, and make not provision for the flesh, to fulfil the lusts thereof," (Romans 13:14).

THE CHRISTIAN WALK
(Romans 8:4; Ps. 1:1; Eph. 4:17; Gen. 6:9; 17:1; Deut. 28:9; Micah 6:8; Rom. 13:13).

The new life of the Christian is described as walking in the Spirit. 'Walking in the Spirit' is a phrase that practically explains the Christian's:
Obedience
Conduct
Behaviour
Lifestyle

It describes the aggregate of the life of the Christian. Jesus used the description of walking to show us the obedience of the Christian. "Then spake Jesus again unto them, saying, I am the light of the world: he that followeth me shall not walk in darkness, but shall have the light of life" (John 8:12). Walking, in a sense, is synonymous with keeping the commandment of the Lord.
The Christian is to;
Walk honestly (Romans 13:13)
Walk by faith (2 Cor. 5:7)

Walk worthy of the Lord (2 Thess. 2:12)
Walk in the light (1 John 1:7)
Walk in the truth (3 John 3, 4)
Walk in love (Eph, 5:2)
Walk in the newness of life (Rom. 6:1).

THE CHARACTERISTICS OF UNREGENERATE PEOPLE

(Romans 8:5-8; 1 Cor. 2:14; John 3:6; James 4:4).

"For they that are after the flesh do mind the things of the flesh; but they that are after the Spirit the things of the Spirit. For to be carnally minded is death; but to be spiritually minded is life and peace" (Romans 8:5, 6).

Here we have four characteristics that mark out the unregenerate and unbelieving from the Spirit-controlled people:

- The first and the most striking character of the unregenerate is that they are after the flesh.
- Second, they are carnally minded. This means they yield to the propensity of the flesh - the carnal mind. They make a practice of the base things of the world.
- Third, they are not subject or submissive to the law of God. They are opposed to the things of God. Something within their hearts revolts against everything that is God.
- Fourth, they cannot please God. They may fast, attend Church services, give alms, pray and engage in seemingly Christian activities but they cannot please God.

These unregenerate who are empty of Christ, grace, and spiritual strength can only be compared with an empty sack that can never stand on its own. They cannot please or serve God. The only thing they are capable of doing is to indulge in corruption.

The unregenerate, natural man receives none of the things of the Spirit of God. They argue against the new birth, the new life in Christ, the inspiration of Scripture, the doctrine of the Bible, holiness, and virtue. They rather defend sin and oppose the saints. They receive not the things of the Spirit of God. They defend worldliness and see nothing wrong in evil.

"For many walk, of whom I have told you often, and now tell you even weeping, that they are the enemies of the cross of Christ," (Phil. 3:18). They think of pleasure more than they think of God. They conveniently give up God and cling to the world. Peter the Apostle gives them a picturesque description. "Having eyes full of adultery, and that cannot cease from sin; beguiling unstable souls: a heart they have exercised with covetous practices; cursed children," (2 Peter 2:14).

The cue here is unmistakeable. If we will really get to know and serve the Lord, we must give up the things of the flesh because the flesh corrupts. Obedience to the Lord is possible only after we are saved and justified. Justification brings transformation and reformation. We cannot save ourselves. It can only be done through the Lord Jesus Christ. "Can the Ethiopian change his skin or the leopard its spots? Then may ye also do good, that are accustomed to do evil," (Jer. 13:23).

GOD'S SPIRIT DWELLING IN ALL BELIEVERS
(Rom. 8:9-13; 1 Cor. 6:19, 20; Gal. 4:6; 5:16).

"But ye are not in the flesh, but in the Spirit, if so be that the Spirit of God dwell in you. Now if any man have not the Spirit of Christ, he is none of his," (Romans 8:9).

The focus here is on all believers – as many as believe on the name of the Lord. Before the Cross, Christ had assured that He, "will pray the Father, and he shall give you another

Comforter, that he may abide with you forever," (John 14:16). In view of this promise, some believers think or believe that the Holy Spirit begins to indwell a person only after the Holy Spirit baptism. But this is not true. As soon as you accept the Lord and get born again, the Holy Spirit begins to indwell you. "Even the Spirit of truth; whom the world cannot receive, because it seeth him not, neither knoweth him: but ye know him; for he dwelleth with you, and shall be in you," (John 14:17). At sanctification, He comes in, in a greater measure and increases more at the experience of Holy Spirit baptism. The Spirit's anointing, fire, unction, and power attends the baptism of the Holy Spirit.

As the Lord makes for the Holy Spirit to indwell the believer, it is imperative that the believer too will create a conducive environment for the Holy Spirit in his life. The commandment to Christians is "put ye on the Lord Jesus Christ, and make not provision for the flesh, to fulfil the lusts thereof," (Romans 13:14). To live in the flesh is to die. "Let us walk honestly, as in the day," (Romans 13:13).

This is instructive for the Romans then and also for all believers in all generations. Some people claim and erroneously teach that 'once saved, always saved'. They couch their thought in fascinating and apparently plausible phrases. They teach that a Christian can still be in the flesh and live in sin. 'Whatever a Christian does, they affirm, is insignificant. Once saved, even if you go back to sin, you will only lose your reward; you cannot lose your relationship with God'. This is unscriptural, false, and baseless. "For if ye live after the flesh, ye shall die: but if ye through the Spirit do mortify the deeds of the body, ye shall live," (Romans 8:13). To be a bible believer, you must always allow the Spirit of God to be in control of your life. The strength of the Spirit of God must be allowed to work in you, mortify the deeds of the body, and make you to live.

"Know ye not that ye are the temple of God, and that the

Spirit of God dwelleth in you? If any man defile the temple of God, him shall God destroy; for the temple of God is holy, which temple ye are," (1 Cor. 3:16, 17).

When we walk in the Spirit of God, there is abundant flourishing of the fruit of the Spirit. "But the fruit of the Spirit is love, joy, peace, longsuffering, gentleness, goodness, faith, meekness, temperance: against such there is no law. And they that are Christ's have crucified the flesh with the affections and lusts. If we live in the Spirit, let us also walk in the Spirit," (Gal. 5:22-25).

Dare Osatimehin

14

THE SPIRIT'S MINISTRY IN THE BELIEVER'S LIFE

Roman 8: 14-30
It is not the possession of extraordinary gifts that makes extraordinary usefulness, but the dedication of what we have to God.

Romans 8:14 - For as many as are led by the Spirit of God, these are sons of God
Romans 8:15 - For ye have not received a spirit of bondage again for fear, but ye have received a spirit of adoption, whereby we cry, Abba, Father
Romans 8:16 - The Spirit itself bears witness with our spirit, that we are children of God
Romans 8:17 - And if children, heirs also: heirs of God, and Christ's joint heirs; if indeed we suffer with him, that we may also be glorified with him
Romans 8:18 - For I reckon that the sufferings of this present time are not worthy to be compared with the coming glory to be revealed to us
Romans 8:19 - For the anxious looking out of the creature expects the Rev. of the sons of God
Romans 8:20 - for the creature has been made subject to vanity, not of its will, but by reason of him who has subjected the same , in hope
Romans 8:21 - that the creature itself also shall be set free from the bondage of corruption into the liberty of the glory of the children of God
Romans 8:22 - For we know that the whole creation groans together and travails in pain together until now
Romans 8:23 - And not only that , but even we ourselves, who have the first-fruits of the Spirit, we also ourselves groan in

ourselves, awaiting adoption, that is the redemption of our body

Romans 8:24 - For we have been saved in hope; but hope seen is not hope; for what any one sees, why does he also hope?

Romans 8:25 - But if what we see not we hope, we expect in patience

Romans 8:26 - And in like manner the Spirit joins also its help to our weakness; for we do not know what we should pray for as is fitting, but the Spirit itself makes intercession with groanings which cannot be uttered

Romans 8:27 - But he who searches the hearts knows what is the mind of the Spirit, because he intercedes for saints according to God

Romans 8:28 - But we do know that all things work together for good to those who love God, to those who are called according to purpose

Romans 8:29 - Because whom he has foreknown, he has also pre-destinated to be conformed to the image of his Son, so that he should be the firstborn among many brethren

Romans 8:30 - But whom he has pre-destinated, these also he has called; and whom he has called, these also he has justified; but whom he has justified, these also he has glorified

In this chapter, we still see the place, position, and power of the Holy Spirit in the life of the believer. The Holy Spirit was active in the initial creation and He is still actively involved in the recreation and redemption of man. The Holy Spirit was central to the earthly ministry of Jesus Christ. He is equally important and indispensable in the life of the Christian. Many Christians do not have adequate knowledge and understanding of the Spirit's ministry in the life of the believer.

On one hand, a group of believers pay lip service to the presence of the Spirit of God in the life of a believer without appropriating His power in their lives. Another group of believers, generally the Pentecostals, seek the gifts of the Spirit without giving enough attention to the fruit of the Spirit in their lives. Whichever group one belongs to, the central truth that runs through all the books of the bible is that the Holy Spirit is the gracious strength of the believer's life. His ministry in the believer's life results in Christ-likeness and holiness of life and conduct.

THE HERITAGE OF GOD'S CHILDREN
(Romans 8:14-17; Gal. 4:5, 6; John 16:7).

"For as many as are led by the Spirit of God, they are the sons of God. For ye have not received the spirit of bondage again to fear; but ye have received the Spirit of adoption, whereby we cry, Abba, Father," (Romans 8:14, 15).

The Holy Spirit begins His lifelong ministry in our lives from the time we are convicted of sin and led to pray for forgiveness and salvation. Without the Holy Spirit, there would not be any conviction or desire to pray or even desire for salvation. "Nevertheless I tell you the truth; It is expedient for you that I go away: for if I go not away, the Comforter will not come unto you; but if I depart, I will send him unto you. And when he is come, he will reprove the world of sin, and of righteousness, and of judgment: Of sin, because they believe not on me; Of righteousness, because I go to my father, and ye see me no more; Of judgement, because the prince of this world is judged," (John 16:7-11).

And till we have our final and ultimate entry into heaven, the ministry of the Holy Spirit in the believer will continue. The Holy Spirit removes the fears of the Christian and assures us of our adoption into the family of God. He alone bears witness with our hearts concerning our sonship. He also leads us day by day into the perfect will of God. From the time we become part of God's family, the Holy Spirit helps us in prayer and makes us to know or possess our inheritance in the Lord. As believers, He makes us to recognise our filial relationship with the Lord and see ourselves as joint-heirs with Christ. He makes us beneficiaries of the Spirit ministry of guidance, help, and intercession, and citizens of the kingdom of Christ.

Thus we see that the believer begins his Christian journey when the Spirit of God begins to bear in his heart that he is a child of God (Romans 8:16). This begins immediately after there is sincere confession, repentance and forsaking of sin in the heart of the repentant soul. This is what John forcefully expressed both in his gospel and his general epistle. "But as many as received him, to them gave he power to become the sons of God, even to them that believe on his name," (John 1:12). "Behold what manner of love the Father hath bestowed upon us, that we should be called the sons of God: therefore the world knoweth us not, because it knew him not. Beloved, now are we the sons of God and it doth not yet appear what we shall be: but we know that, when he shall appear, we shall be like him; for we shall see him as he is. And every man that hath this hope in him purifieth himself, even as he is pure," (1 John 3:1-3).

Second, we are adopted into the family of God (Romans 8:15). This adoption draws us into a very intimate relationship. We become children – sons and daughters of God and look at Him as the Father, not a Judge. The sacrifice of His Son has gotten rid of our sins and iniquities and we now know that there is no condemnation to us because we are in His Son, Christ Jesus. We no longer live in fear. We are on the side of the Lord and we boldly come before the throne of grace. "For God hath not given us the spirit of fear; but of power, and of love, and of a sound mind," (2 Tim. 1:7).

And sequel to our new relationship with the Lord, He now leads or guides us by His Spirit. That is why the Apostle says: "For as many as are led by the Spirit of God, they are the sons of God," (Roman 8:14). This is the heritage or inheritance of the children of God. Saints in the Old Testament cherished the leading of the Spirit of God. They enjoyed this in the wilderness through the symbolic ministry of the pillar of cloud by day and pillar of fire by night. The prophets and Psalmist alluded several times to the leading and guidance of the Lord. "Thus saith the Lord, thy redeemer, the Holy One of Israel I am the LORD thy God which teacheth thee to profit, which leadeth thee by the way that thou shouldest go," (Isaiah 48:17).

The unbelievers are led by the tradition and ways of men, bad examples around them, the devil and their carnal minds. But the children of God are led by the Lord, examples of holy men in scriptures, the workings, instructions and commandments in scriptures and the Holy Spirit. The Spirit of God reveals the mind of God to the sincere seeker, thereby guides, and leads him. It is only those who are being led continually by the Holy Spirit that are evidently the sons or daughters of God.

HEIRS OF GOD
(1 Cor 2:9, 10, 12).

"And if children then heirs; heirs of God and joint-heirs with Christ" (Romans 8:17a)."

The concept of heirs here is vividly grasped by Old Testament saints. Isaac was Abraham's heir and everything including God's promises was bequeathed to him. Esau lost his heritage because he sold his birth right to Jacob who became Isaac's heir and had everything including God's promises bequeathed to him. Jacob gave a great inheritance to his children.

Today, our inheritance in Christ is beyond description. Our human language cannot fully explore or explain what it means to be joint-heirs with Christ. To be heirs of God means to be joint-heirs with Christ. Being heirs of God means much for us here on earth and much more for us in heaven. Men's finite mind and faculties cannot comprehend this infinite inheritance of children of God. All of God's are ours and they are revealed to us by His Spirit. Christians are not to live orphaned and destitute here on earth. We should know our rights and possess them. To be sure, we will not get or possess all our inheritance here on earth. There is a part we will get when we arrive in heaven. It is in view of this great inheritance in heaven that the Lord encourages us to endure till the end.

INEXPRESSIBLE GROAN FOR INDESCRIBABLE GLORY
(Rom 8:17, 19; Phil 3:20, 21; Col 3:4; 2 Thess2:14-16; 1 Peter 1:7, 8; 4:13; 5:1).

"...If so be that we suffer with him, that we may be also glorified together," (Rom 8:17).
This scripture introduces us to two concept;
- The concept of suffering
- The concept of being glorified

The suffering is for the present time; the glory is for the future. Between the time of suffering and the dawn of glory there is a groaning. The groaning heralds the glory. The glory is described as 'the manifestation of the sons of God' (Romans 8:19; 1 John 3:1, 2). The focus is unmistakeable – presently the saint looks ordinary though rich in grace, glory and honour. The people around do not see the full manifestation of that glory. Jesus was also seen ordinarily until Peter declared that He was Jesus, the Son of God. Before the experience of the Mount of Transfiguration, Peter and the other apostles did not see anything extraordinarily glorious about Him. But when they saw His indescribable glory on the Mount of Transfiguration, they could not but ask for its perpetuity (Luke 9:33).

For believers too, there is a coming glory, which will be with all splendour. That is why John later said, "It doth not yet appear what we shall be: but we know that, when he shall appear, we shall be like him; for we shall see him as he is."

From the time of the fall of man, the whole earth had been subjected to a curse. There had been a limitation. The prophets of the Old Testament began to see that a new change was on the way. They saw in vision, the reign of the Lord, the millennial reign and desired its early arrival. Isaiah and the other prophets spoke of this splendour, the loss of the ferocity in animals and the attendant peace of the period; he looked forward to it. But they observed that the whole of creation is subject unto vanity. And humanity is part of this groaning. Our body is groaning now under the yoke of frailty, weariness, sickness, heartaches or infirmity. But our souls and spirits are redeemed.

The pain and agony of birth ceases to be felt as soon as the child is born and the joy of a new child fills the air (John 16:21, 22). In the same vein, all agony and groaning we are having now, will be past and forgotten as soon as we get to heaven. To the disciples, Jesus said the agony, trials and pain they are passing through now with the persecution and misrepresentation from the Jews will cease when He comes back to see them again. Their joy thereafter will have no interruption, though now there are interruptions. Paul the Apostle says it again in his epistle to the Corinthians. "For in this we groan, earnestly desiring to be clothed upon with our house which is from heaven: If so be that being clothed we shall not be found naked. For we that are in this tabernacle do groan, being burdened: not for that we would be unclothed, but clothed upon, that mortality might be swallowed up of life," (2 Cor. 5:2-4).

Our vile bodies will be changed. A new glory will be given to us. Our groaning will give way to glory. Since the time of the fall, the whole creation has been earnestly desirous for a restoration to the original beauty and glory. The coming glory is one of the blessed things of the New Testament. That is why the Apostle, in the seventeenth verse, spoke of our being glorified together with Christ. He also wrote of 'the glory, which shall be revealed in us'. This is the indescribable glory the Church is waiting for. It is referred to as 'the glorious liberty of the children of God', (verse 21) and 'the redemption of our body', (verse 23). It is for this indescribable glory that we patiently wait. And the whole earth is pictured as groaning while waiting. But it is a groaning and waiting that is worth it because a moment spent in eternal glory will obliterate the age or decades spent groaning here. Paul puts this succinctly in his second epistle to the Corinthians. "For our light affliction, which is but for a moment, worketh for us a far more exceeding and eternal weight of glory," (2 Cor. 4:17).

All perplexity, disappointment, disillusionment, lack, poverty or sorrow will look like light affliction when we eventually get to heaven.

To partake of the glory that shall come, the believer must patiently endure the suffering of the present moment. Those who compromise now will suffer throughout eternity. Those who endure now will rejoice and be glorified with Christ throughout eternity. Whatever we suffer now is simply a light affliction. We shall rejoice with joy unspeakable, full of glory. The Lord encourages us to patiently wait for it (Romans 8:24, 25).

THE SPIRIT'S ASSISTANCE FROM JUSTIFICATION TO GLORIFICATION
(Romans 8:26-30)

"Likewise the Spirit also helpeth our infirmities: for we know not what we should pray for as we ought: but the Spirit itself maketh intercession for us with groaning which cannot be uttered," (Romans 8:26).

Here the Apostle brings to the fore the weakness of the

Church. He shows how weak our understanding is, how spineless our desires in the things of God are and eventually how weak our prayers have become. The Holy Spirit then helps us in prayer and makes intercession for us with inexpressible groaning. The indwelling Spirit helps the believer to pray according to the will of God; its expansion, extension, the deepening of its members, the needs of the members of the body of Christ is missing at times, and the Holy Spirit comes in to assist us to vocalise this unknown burden. The believer, if left alone, cannot pray and plan according to the will of God. But when the Holy Spirit helps us, we begin to pray, plan and work according to the will of God because he knows the mind of God (Romans 8:27).

ALL THINGS WORK TOGETHER FOR GOOD (Romans 8:28)

We will never know that all the things that happen to us are according to the will of God except the Spirit of God enlightens us. Sarah asked God why she could not have a child. Abraham wondered aloud if the servant of his house would be his heir. Rachael told Jacob to give her children lest she died. It is only the Spirit of God that can help us to see the wisdom and finger of God in our situations. With the illumination, the comfort and the counsel of the Holy Spirit, we shall ultimately know that all things – favour or disappointments, poverty or riches, wealth or want – work together for good to them that love God and are the called according to His purpose.

15

FALLACY OF THE DOCTRINE OF PREDESTINATION

And we know that all things work together for good to them that love God, to them who are the called according to his purpose (Romans 8:28)

People generally misunderstand this scripture. They employ it to back up the doctrine of predestination. They therefore seek to remove the onus of responsibility for the sinner's action off him. They say, some people are congenitally, predestined some to be saved and some to be lost. This, they further claim, is an act of God. But this is false because the Bible says God is not willing that any should perish but that all should come to repentance (2 Peter 3:9). He will have all men to be saved. "God so loved the world that He gave his only begotten Son that whosoever believeth in Him will not perish but have everlasting life" (John 3:16). "Whosoever will let him come and take of the water of life freely" (Rev 22:17). "Come now, and let us reason together, saith the LORD: though your sins be as scarlet, they shall be as white as snow, though they be red like crimson, they shall be as wool. If ye be willing and obedient, ye shall eat the good of the land," (Isaiah 1:18-19).

This scripture, therefore, speaks of the foreknowledge of God. He has called all but only a few are chosen (Matt. 22:14). He desires that all come unto Him. But in view of the free will of men, all would not come; they would prefer the pleasure of sin and indulge in it. God knows those who will respond excitedly and embrace Calvary. He knows those who will spun the efforts of the Lord. How? "Known unto God are all his works from the foundation of the world," (Acts 15:18).

Those who respond to God's call are, in God's design and goal, to be conformed to the image of His Son. He wants all His children to be Holy and Christ like. He has so ordained that as soon as you come into the body of Christ all the means of grace and privileges to be holy and conformed to the image of God is available for you to employ.

CALLED, JUSTIFIED AND GLORIFIED
(Romans 8:29, 30)

Those who eventually respond to the call of God will be justified and those who are justified will be glorified. Only those who accept the Lord, repent of their sins and follow the Lord are justified. Those who keep on the faith till the end will be glorified. Jesus taught this truth and affirmed it. The beauty of it is that we have the help and aid of the Holy Spirit, to see us through and assist us to continue with the Lord till the end.

HELL – THE DESTINY OF THE SINNER

Too many people seem to expect that hell will be as much fun as the path leading there.

Matt. 25:41- Then shall he say also unto them on the left hand, Depart from me, ye cursed, into everlasting fire, prepared for the devil and his angels

Matt. 25:46 - And these shall go away into everlasting punishment: but the righteous into life eternal.

Mark 9:43 - And if thy hand offend thee, cut it off: it is better for thee to enter into life maimed, than having two hands to go into hell, into the fire that never shall be quenched
Mark 9:44 - Where their worm dieth not and the fire is not quenched.
Mark 9:45 - And if thy foot offend thee, cut it off: it is better for thee to enter halt into life, than having two feet to be cast into hell, into the fire that never shall be quenched
Mark 9:46 - Where their worm dieth not, and the fire is not quenched
Mark 9:47 - And if thine eye offend thee, pluck it out: it is better for thee to enter into the kingdom of God with one eye, than having two eyes to be cast into hell fire
Mark 9:48 - Where their worm dieth not, and the fire is not quenched.

Luke 16:22 - And it came to pass, that the beggar died, and was carried by the angels into Abraham's bosom: the rich man also died, and was buried
Luke 16:23 - And in hell he lift up his eyes, being in torments, and seeth Abraham afar off, and Lazarus in his bosom
Luke 16:24 - And he cried and said, Father Abraham, have mercy on me, and send Lazarus, that he may dip the tip of his finger in water, and cool my tongue; for I am tormented in this flame
Luke 16:25 - But Abraham said, Son, remember that thou in thy lifetime receivedst thy good things, and likewise Lazarus evil things: but now he is comforted, and thou art tormented
Luke 16:26 - And beside all this, between us and you there is a great gulf fixed: so that they which would pass from hence to you cannot; neither can they pass to us that would come from

thence
Luke 16:27 - Then he said, I pray thee therefore, father, that thou wouldest send him to my father's house
Luke 16:28 - For I have five brethren; that he may testify unto them, lest they also come into this place of torment.

Rev. 20:13 - And the sea gave up the dead which were in it; and death and hell delivered up the dead which were in them: and they were judged every man according to their works
Rev. 20:14 - And death and hell were cast into the lake of fire. This is the second death
Rev. 20:15 - And whosoever was not found written in the book of life was cast into the lake of fire
Rev. 21:8 - But the fearful, and unbelieving, and the abominable, and murderers, and whoremongers, and sorcerers, and idolaters, and all liars, shall have their part in the lake which burneth with fire and brimstone: which is the second death.

Hell: Derived from the Saxon helan which means to cover, hence the covered or the invisible place. In the Scripture there are three words so rendered:
(1) Sheol, occurring in the Old Testament sixty-five times. This word Sheol is derived from a root-word meaning 'to ask' or 'demand,' hence insatiableness (Pro 30:15, Pro 30:16). It is rendered 'grave' thirty-one times (Gen 37:35; Gen 42:38; Gen 44:29, Gen 44:31; 1Sa 2:6, etc.). The revisers have retained this rendering in the historical books with the original word in the margin, while in the poetical books, they have reversed this rule. In thirty-one cases in the Authorized Version this word is rendered 'hell' - the place of disembodied spirits. The inhabitants of Sheol are 'the congregation of the dead' (Pro 21:16). It is: the abode of the wicked (Num 16:33; Job 24:19; Psa 9:17; Psa 31:17, etc.) and; of the good (Psalm 16:10; Psa

30:3; Psa 49:15; Psa 86:13, etc.). Sheol is described as: deep (Job 11:8), dark (Job 10:21, Job 10:22), with bars (Job 17:16) and the dead 'go down' to it (Num 16:30, Num 16:33; Ezekiel 31:15, Ezek 31:16, Ezek 31:17).

(2) The Greek word Hades of the New Testament has the same scope of signification as Sheol of the Old Testament. It is a prison (1Pet 3:19), with gates and bars and locks (Mat 16:18; Rev 1:18), and it is downward (Mat.11:23; Luke 10:15). The righteous and the wicked are separated. The blessed dead are in that part of Hades called paradise (Luke 23:43). They are also said to be in Abraham's bosom (Luke 16:22).

(3) Gehenna in most of its occurrences in the Greek New Testament, designates the place of the lost (Mat 23:33). The fearful nature of their condition there is described in various figurative expressions (Mat 8:12; Mat 13:42; Mat 22:13; Mat 25:30; Luke 16:24, etc.).

What is Hinnom? A deep, narrow ravine separating Mount Zion from the so-called 'Hill of Evil Counsel.' It took its name from an ancient hero, 'the son of Hinnom'. It is first mentioned in Joshua 15:8 as the place where the idolatrous Jews burned their children alive to Moloch and Baal. A particular part of the valley was called Tophet, or the 'fire-stove,' where the children were burned. After the exile, in order to show their abhorrence of the locality, the Jews made this valley the receptacle of the offal of the city, for the destruction, of which a fire was, as is supposed, kept constantly burning there. The Jews associated with this valley these two ideas: that of the sufferings of the victims that had there been sacrificed; and that of filth and corruption

It therefore became popular to the mind a symbol of the

abode of the wicked. It came to signify hell as the place of the wicked. It might be shown by infinite examples that the Jews expressed hell or the place of the damned, by this word. The word Gehenna [the Greek contraction of Hinnom] was never used in the time of Christ in any other sense than to denote the place of future punishment. About this fact there can be no question. In this sense the word is used eleven times in our Lord's discourses (Mat 23:33; Luke 12:5; Mat 5:22, etc.).

1. THE CERTAINTY OF HELL

Hell is a place of torment, of eternal and everlasting punishment in unquenchable fire (Matt. 25:41-46; Mark 9:43-48; Luke 16:23, 24, and 28). Hell is real; yes it is real. As certain as heaven is, so is the certainty of Hell. Its punishment is eternal as God Himself. Eternity is like lifting up your eyes to look at the sky, the more you look, the more you see but when your eyes have stopped seeing, eternity has just started. It is like going to the ocean and using a bucket to empty the water, when you have stopped emptying all the waters in the ocean to another place, eternity has just started. God is real, His words are real and eternal, so are all His creatures.

A. REFERENCES IN THE OLD TESTAMENT

Deut. 32:22; Psalm 9:17; 86:13; Prov. 7:24-27; 9:13-18; 15:24; Prov. 23:14; Isaiah 5:14-16; 14:15; 28:18, 19; 30:33; 33:14.

Eternal punishment is not a pleasant subject for discussion, yet it is a fearful reality, an awful state and a tragic fate. If we are to preach and teach the word faithfully, we must not omit the facts about hell. To know that hell awaits the impenitent and to keep silent on the matter would be injustice to mankind. We are to teach the total word to the total man.

B. THE TEACHING OF JESUS:

Jesus' teaching on hell was as clear and precise as it will ever

be. He warned all believers and the whole world of:
The danger of Hell. Matt. 5:22, 9, 30; 10:28; 18:8,9; Mark 9:43-48; Luke 12:5.
Everlasting Punishment. Matt. 25:41, 46; Mark 9:43-48; Luke 16:22-28; Rev. 14:10, 11.
Abode of sinners who die unsaved. Matt. 7:15-19; 23:33; 25:41-46; Luke 16:23; Rev. 19:20; Rev. 20:14, 15; 21:8.
You will be surprised that Jesus spoke more about Hell in the Bible than about Heaven.

C. THE APOSTLES' DOCTRINE
Romans 2:5-9; 2 Thess. 1:8, 9; Hebrews 10:26,27; James 3:5,6; 2 Peter 2:4,9; 3:7; Jude 7,23; See also Matt. 3:7-10.

We are to interpret Old Testament terms by the New Testament meaning put into them. By the later usage of the New Testament, the Holy Spirit shows us what He meant by the usage of the Old Testament. Also the words of the prophets and the apostles are to be interpreted by the clear, plain teachings of Jesus Christ.

Although it will be nice to believe that people get a second chance or that hell is only temporary, there are no scriptures from the Bible to indicate this. Hell is a place of eternal punishment, unquenchable and everlasting fire. Hell is a place where no one wants to go ... and you don't have to.

2. THE NATURE AND FINALITY OF HELL

There are some errors taught among some denominations and cults. These errors give false hope to multitudes. Many will be disappointed as they will see and know the truth about hell and feel its reality when there will be no more chance to repent. Many people believe that a good and loving God would not want to send anyone to hell. This is true, for God's desire is that 'none shall perish but all to come to repentance'. However, God offers to everyone the gift of eternal life with Him in Heaven and not in hell, by their choice of receiving Jesus Christ into their lives.

COMMON ERRORS

A. Annihilation of the wicked: The Jehovah's Witnesses and the Seventh Day Adventists teach that sinners will be burnt up in hell. This is false. The fire and punishments of hell is eternal and everlasting. It burns with fire and brimstone but the inhabitants are not consumed. You don't want and have to be in hell. Note: Scripture declare the future punishment of the wicked to be eternal. In the great majority of scripture passages on the future punishment of sinners, they signify 'everlasting'. The same words, 'everlasting' and 'eternal are used to express the eternal duration of God, the Father, Son and Holy Spirit (Romans 16:26; I Tim. 1:17; Hebrews 9:14; Rev. 1:18. See also John 14:17; Matt. 19:29; 2 Cor. 9:9). The same word is used in Matt. 25:46 to describe both the sufferings of the wicked and the happiness of the righteous. Therefore it is clear that the misery of the lost is eternal in the same sense as the life of God or the blessedness of the saved is eternal.

The words 'perish, destroy, destruction and lost,' when used in connection with future punishment do not mean annihilation or cessation of being on the part of the wicked. For 'perish' in Luke 13:2-5; John 3:16 see Esther 4:16; Isaiah 57:1, 2; Daniel 9:26; Acts 13:41. For 'destroy or destruction' in I Thess. 1:8, 9 see I Cor. 3:17; 2 Cor. 7:2; 2 Peter 3:7, compare Matt. 10:28 with Luke 12:4, 5. In both Testaments, death is shown to be the termination of man's earthly existence, but not an extinction of his being or his consciousness.

B. Purgatory: This is Catholic superstition of suffering in the intermediate state. This is also false and a fallacy. It is appointed unto man to die once and after that judgment, so the Holy Bible says.

Dare Osatimehin

16

THE GREAT WHITE THRONE OF JUDGMENT

Rev. 20:11-15

It is good to be saved and know it, but it is better to be saved and show it and it is best to be saved and remain saved till eternity

"And I saw a great white throne, and him that sat on it ... and the dead were judged." This gives the account of the final judgment and what a solemn, sobering, serious passage it is! The first time the Apostle John saw a throne and the One who sat on it was in Rev. chapter 4.

The contrast between that throne and this great white throne is striking and instructive. "Behold, a throne was set in heaven, and one sat on the throne ... and there was a rainbow round about the throne ... and out of the throne proceeded lightnings and thunderings and voices ... and (they) give glory and honour and thanks to him that sat on the throne ... and worship him." In chapter 4 there was the rainbow, a sign of the faithfulness of the merciful, covenant-keeping God. In chapter 20 there was no rainbow around the judgment throne. There is nothing but justice and retribution.

What an awesome hour it will be! In chapter 4, there were lightnings and thunderings of warning. In chapter 20, there were no warnings since the day of grace had passed forever! In chapter 4, there was worship and there was singing around the throne. In chapter 20, no singing, only the awful silence of the damned and the doomed. The final reckoning day of judgment had come! What a day that would be! Where will you be?

1. THE FAITHFUL AND FIERCE JUDGE
Rev. 20:11; Psalms 9:7,8,16,17; 97:2-7; Daniel 7:9,10; Acts 17:30,31; Eccl. 12:13,14; Romans 2:16; 2 Thess. 1:8,9; 2 Peter 3:7,10-12; Hebrews 12:25-29; 10:27-31; Romans 1:28-32.

"And I saw a great white throne." This is a throne of judgment - the final judgment. All people from all nations and all generations who refused to come before the throne of grace to receive mercy and salvation will come before the throne of judgment. It is a great throne - the throne of the great God, the Most High, and the great Judge from whom no one can escape. A great, exalted, high throne of the final judgment of the last day! And it is a white, bright, shining, dazzling throne from where spotless, flawless, faultless, irreversible justice will come forth.

"And him that sat on it." Who sits on this awe-inspiring throne? "The Father hath committed all judgment unto the Son." "It is he which was ordained of God to be the Judge of quick and dead." "God shall judge the secrets of men by Jesus Christ." "The Son of man shall come in his glory, then shall he sit upon the throne of his glory: And before him shall be gathered all nations" (John 5:22; Acts 10:42; Romans 2:16; Matt. 25:31, 32). It will be a fearful, frightening sight as the earth and the heaven, -the earthly elements and heavenly firmament- will flee away. What fright as sinners stand alone before the great Judge! There will be no escape.

2. THE FINAL AND FAIR JUDGMENT
Rev. 20:12, 13; Daniel 12:2; John 5:28, 29; Acts 24:15; Eccl. 11:9; John 3:18-20; Psalm 28:4, 5; Prov. 24:12; Jer. 17:9, 10;

32:19; Romans 2:5-11; Rev. 2:20-23.

"And I saw the dead, small and great, stand before God." All the dead who have not taken part in the resurrection at the time of the rapture and also at the beginning of Christ's Millennial Reign will now rise from the dead to stand before the great Judge (1 Thess. 4:14-17; Rev. 20:4-6). The dead, small and great, young and old, rich and poor, men and women, bound and free, educated and illiterate, leaders and laity, the pulpit and the pew, the ruler and the ruled who have not taken part in the resurrection of the just will now be raised from the dead to stand before the Judge on the throne for the final judgment. It will be immaterial how long you have been dead, or the circumstances surrounding your death and place of death, all shall rise up to face the judgement.

"And the books were opened ... and the dead were judged out of those things which were written in the books, according to their works."

The books refer to the books of records containing the records of all human deeds. The records will constitute the basis of the final judgment on the last day. The all-seeing God takes note of all the deeds, actions, evil and idle words, motives and lives of all individuals on earth. Those who were once saints in the church but sinners outside shall face the public shame. The final judgment will not be arbitrary and will not be determined by man's rank, position, status or profession. It will be based on the record of men's secret acts and total influence of character. What a day that will be when God will evaluate each man's deeds and determine his eternal destiny! Then all will know that the secrets of men are all but an open scandal in the court of heaven. All unconfessed sins and thoughts of evil will be judged. All the inappropriate actions, miscarried judgement and justice, the words of prophecies that men have said in the name of God when God did not send them will be judged. What an awful spectacle it will be for those men of God in quote that cherish their position instead of holding firm their biblical stand and beliefs. Those who had used the name of God to enrich themselves with money, material and position will finally meet their doom. Alas! There will be no escape.

3. THE FATHOMLESS AND FRIGHTFUL JUSTICE

Rev. 20:14, 15; 1 Cor. 15:26; Isaiah 25:8; Hosea 13:14; Rev. 14:9-11; 19:20; 20:10; 21:8; Matt. 13:40-42, 49, 50; 25:41, 46; Mark 9:43-48; Luke 16:23-26.

Rev. 20:14 - And death and hell were cast into the lake of fire. This is the second death

Rev. 20:15 - And whosoever was not found written in the book of life was cast into the lake of fire.

Rev. 14:9 - And the third angel followed them, saying with a loud voice, If any man worship the beast and his image, and receive his mark in his forehead, or in his hand

Rev.14:10 - The same shall drink of the wine of the wrath of God, which is poured out without mixture into the cup of his indignation; and he shall be tormented with fire and brimstone in the presence of the holy angels, and in the presence of the Lamb

Rev. 14:11 - And the smoke of their torment ascendeth up for ever and ever: and they have no rest day nor night, who worship the beast and his image, and whosoever receiveth the mark of his name.

Rev. 21:8 - But the fearful, and unbelieving, and the abominable, and murderers, and whoremongers, and sorcerers, and idolaters, and all liars, shall have their part in the lake which burneth with fire and brimstone: which is the second death.

"And death and hell were cast into the lake of fire …The last enemy that shall be destroyed is death." Death, considered as the separation of soul and body will exist no more. The reign of death would come to an end. The righteous will live for ever with God in heaven and the unrighteous will live forever in the lake of fire, forever separated from God.

"And whosoever was not found written in the book of life was cast into the lake of fire." The single condition that would save anyone from being cast into the lake of fire is to be "found written in the book of life." All others, princes, kings, nobles, philosophers, politicians, atheists, musicians, statesmen, conquerors; rich men and poor men; the young and the aged; the humble and the proud, the sober and the vain; the religious and the atheist - whosoever was not found written in the book of life was cast into the lake of fire. The rich men will be there but the wealth and the prosperity will have melted away; the pauper will be there too, but there debt will be too heavy to pay, the widow and the orphans will be there , the drunkard and the gambler will not be left behind, the man that sold them the drink and the man that gave them the license, will all face the judgment of God. The moral man and the self-righteous, the people that have scorned the gospel message saying, "not tonight, I will get saved bye and bye, I don't have time for religion," will eventually have time to die and appear before God.

Where will you be? How can and will you be saved if you neglect so great a salvation that God has wrought through His only begotten Son, Jesus? It is never too late. Repent now and believe the gospel of peace for it is a fearful thing to fall into the hand of the mighty God.

The Great Judgment Morning

1. I dreamed that the great judgment morning
   Had dawned and the trumpet had blown;
   I dreamed that the nations had gathered
   To judgment before the white throne;
   From the throne came a bright shining angel,
   And stood on the land and the sea,
   And swore with his hand raised to heaven,
   That time was no longer to be.

Chorus
And O, what a weeping and wailing,
As the lost were told of their fate;
They cried for the rocks and the mountains,
They prayed, but their prayer was too late.

2. The rich man was there, but his money
   Had melted and vanished away;
   A pauper he stood in the judgment,
   His debts were too heavy to pay;
   The great man was there, but his greatness,
   When death came, was left far behind!
   The angel that opened the records,
   Not a trace of his greatness could find

3. The widow was there with the orphans,
   God heard and remembered their cries;
   No sorrow in heaven for ever,
   God wiped all the tears from their eyes;
   The gambler was there and the drunkard,

And the man that had sold them the drink,
With the people who gave him the license,
Together in hell they did sink.

4. The moral man came to the judgment,
But his self-righteous rags would not do;
The men who had crucified Jesus
Had passed off as moral men, too;
The soul that had put off salvation,
"Not tonight; I'll get saved by and by,
No time now to think of religion!"
At last they had found time to die.

17

FREE AND NEVER TO BE BOUND

Jer. 34:8-11
Freedom is not the right to do as you please,
But the liberty to do as you ought

Jer. 34:8 - The word that came unto Jer. from Jehovah, after that king Zedekiah had made a covenant with all the people that were at Jerusalem, to proclaim liberty unto them
Jer. 34:9 - That every man should let his bondman, and every man his bondmaid, the Hebrew and the Hebrewess, go free, that none should exact service of them, that is, of a Jew his brother
Jer. 34:10 - And all the princes and all the people that had entered into the covenant obeyed, every man letting his bondman and every man his bondmaid go free, that none should exact service of them any more: they obeyed, and let them go
Jer. 34:11 - But afterwards they turned, and caused the bondmen and the bondmaids whom they had let go free, to return, and brought them into subjection for bondmen and for bondmaids

Complete freedom is real, yet some people do not experience it. Rather than being totally free, they go through a vicious circle of ups and downs, hot and cold, victory and defeat, success and demotion, forward and backward movements. After being healed and made healthy, saved and sanctified, victorious and vibrant; after being made to stand in freedom, the believer should never be bound again. This desirable kind of freedom guarantees that the recipient remains free from sin, servitude, self, sorcery, secret societies, snares, and spirits of the devil and Satan. The God-kind of freedom is one that lasts and lasts forever if you remain in Him.

Many people do not care about the aftermath or afterward of a current experience of freedom as the euphoria of their present experience of freedom makes them forget that they could lose it and become captives again. The experience of the Jewish menservants and maidservants illustrates this. The declaration and covenant to let those in servitude go free was initially obeyed by Jewish masters. "But afterward they turned, and caused the servants and the handmaids, whom they had let go free, to return, and brought them into subjection for servants and for handmaids." (Jer. 34:11). After receiving salvation, deliverance, healing and other blessings, the believer needs to be careful and concerned about keeping the experience, vowing never to be bound again.

1. PROMISED FREEDOM FOR TRUE CHILDREN OF GOD

John 8:30-32, 36; Matt. 17:26; Romans 8:15, 16, 21; Gal. 3:25, 26.

As Christ proclaimed the message of His gospel, some of His hearers singled themselves out by their attitude and response of believing His word. And by that commendable attitude, they became qualified to enjoy all other benefits of the gospel. Christ recognises such unique people who exercise faith in His word and therefore, concentrates His exhortation and declaration of the gospel blessing to them. It is this group who has started with a decision to believe the gospel that Christ admonishes to continue in His word: "If ye continue in my word, then are ye my disciples indeed; And ye shall know the truth, and the truth shall make you free," (John 8:31, 32). Those who accept and receive His word and have become children of God are those He promised lasting freedom. "If the Son therefore shall make you free, ye shall be free indeed," (John 8:36). This kind of freedom is complete and all-encompassing. True children of God are free in the day and in the night, in the crowd and while alone.

Christ has promised to set everyone free from the bondage to sin, sorcery, secret societies, snares, spirits of the devil and Satan that limits potentials and hinders usefulness in life. Set free by Christ, true children of God do not return to bondage but abide in the glorious liberty of Christ. Faith in Christ sets free from condemnation, crime and conspiracy of the wicked. When the Lord sets free, nothing limits. And the freedom not only gives big dream but also helps to fulfil same. Like an eagle, nothing impedes the journey of such an individual to the envisioned destination and destiny.

2. PERSONAL FREEDOM FOR TRUE CHILDREN OF GOD

Romans 8:1, 2; 7:15-19; John 8:11, 12; Romans 6:6, 7, 18, 22; Titus 2:11-14.

Sin and its guilt in the heart limit usefulness, but the freedom that Christ gives frees from condemnation. This freedom is not just theoretical or pictorial; it is personal and practical. It is the freedom that the blood of the Lamb procured at Calvary for the redemption of man; it is a personal experience that transforms the sinner or backslider. Paul relates his experience of personal freedom. "For the law of the Spirit of life in Christ Jesus hath made me free from the law of sin and death," (Romans 8:1, 2).

Forgiveness of sin and cleansing in the blood of Christ precedes a personal experience of freedom for true children of God. Those who have not tasted this experience of freedom from Christ usually live and talk like prisoners. "For that which I do I allow not: for what I would, that do I not; but what I hate, that do I... Now then it is no more I that do it, but sin that dwelleth in me... for to will is present with me; but how to perform that which is good I find not. For the good that I would I do not: but the evil which I would not, that I do," (Romans 7:15-19). Sin usually brings condemnation to such people until the power of Christ's blood brings pardon and cleansing, and removes every form of condemnation from the heart. Thereafter, the power of Christ's righteousness replaces that of sin, and condemnation for sin is taken away. For everyone who turns away from sin, Christ sets free, not only from sin but also from satanic powers that oppress, hinder progress, cause failure, etc. This experience of personal freedom makes the believer live a holy and righteous lifestyle. And without this experience of freedom from sin, there will be palpable fear whenever the soon return of Christ is mentioned.

3. PERMANENT FREEDOM FOR TRUE CHILDREN OF GOD

Gen. 5:22, 24; 39:7-9; 1 John 5:18; Gal. 5:1.

Enoch had a continual, complete, consistent and permanent experience of freedom from sin; his righteous life and eventual rapture attest to this. Joseph was also righteous. He did not avoid sin for fear of losing his position and privileges or of contracting diseases but because of his freedom from sin. He knew that he was on pilgrimage to God's plan for him, and would not allow sin to hinder him from getting there.

Likewise, the believer does not avoid sin because of the fear of Church discipline or of losing some privileges but because of his freedom from sin. When tempted, every true child of God should ask, like Joseph, "How then can I do this great wickedness, and sin against God?" The believer also has the same purpose of heart and his faith in Christ is devoid of pecuniary reasons. His ultimate desire is to make it to heaven at last. Thus, he lives a life of freedom from sin. In view of the promise of freedom, the presence and power of the indwelling Christ, the purpose of making heaven, and the privilege reserved for the children of God, the believer needs to stand fast therefore in the liberty wherewith Christ hath made us free, and be not entangled again with the yoke of bondage (Gal. 5:1), knowing that Christ sets free and keeps the believer permanently free from sin.

Power In The Blood

1. Would you be free from your burden of sin?
   There's power in the blood, power in the blood;
   Would you o'er evil a victory win?
   There's wonderful power in the blood.

Chorus
There is power, power, wonder-working power
In the blood of the Lamb,
There is power, power, wonder-working power

In the precious blood of the Lamb.

2. Would you be free from your passion and pride?
   There's power in the blood, power in the blood;
   Come for a cleansing to Calvary's tide,
   There's wonderful power in the blood.

3. Would you be whiter, much whiter than snow?
   There's power in the blood, power in the blood;
   Sin stains are lost in its life giving flow,
   There's wonderful power in the blood.

4. Would you do service for Jesus your King?
   There's power in the blood, power in the blood;
   Would you live daily His praises to sing?
   There's wonderful power in the blood.

18

ALCOHOL ANONYMOUS

The maintenance of Ignorance is the strength of the oppressor

Am I an alcoholic?

If you repeatedly drink more than you intend or want to, or if you get into trouble when you drink you may be an alcoholic. Only you can decide. No one will tell you whether you are or not. You need to be very real and sincere to yourself.

STATISTICS

- After smoking, alcoholism kills more people in the United Kingdom than any other drug. One adult in 13 is dependent on drinking, according to Government statistics.
- 33,000 people die each year due to alcohol-related incidents or associated health problems.
- Alcohol is involved in 15% of road accidents, 26% of drowning, and 36% of death in fires.
- A quarter of accidents at work are drink-related.

ALCOHOL DEATHS

- UK rates increase in 2008 -The number of alcohol-related deaths in the United Kingdom has consistently increased since the early 1990s, rising from the lowest figure of 4,023 (6.7 per 100,000) in 1992 to the highest of 9,031 (13.6 per 100,000) in 2008. Although figures in recent years suggested that the trend was leveling out, alcohol-related deaths in males increased further in 2008. Female rates have remained stable.

- There are more alcohol-related deaths in men than in women. The rate of male deaths has more than doubled over the period from 9.1 per 100,000 in 1991 to 18.7 per 100,000 in 2008. There have been steadier increases in female rates, rising from 5.0 per 100,000 in 1991 to 8.7 in 2008, less than half the rate for males. In 2008, males accounted for approximately two-thirds of the total number of alcohol-related deaths. There were 5,999 deaths in men and 3,032 in women.

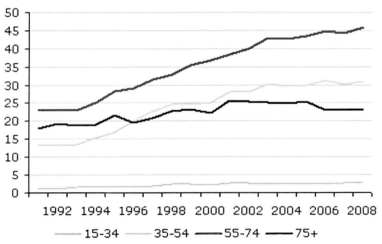

Male alcohol-related death rates by age-group, United Kingdom, 1991-2008

The trends differ according to age. For both males and females, the lowest rates across the period were in those aged 15-34. In 2008, the rates were 2.9 per 100,000 and 1.3 per

100,000 respectively. The highest rates have occurred in persons aged 55-74. In men, the rate has increased from 23.0 per 100,000 in 1992 and 1993 to 45.8 per 100,000 in 2008, the highest rate recorded across all age groups. Alcohol-related deaths in all age groups increased in 2008 compared with figures in 2007.

Alcohol-related death rates among females have been consistently lower than rates for males and trends demonstrate a broadly similar pattern across different age groups. The highest rates for women during the 1991-2008 period were in those aged 55-74. In 2008, the rate for this group peaked at 21.5 per 100,000. Rates in all other age groups decreased slightly and were lowest in women aged 15-34 at 1.3 per 100,000.

Source: Office for National Statistics, General Register Office for Scotland, Northern Ireland Statistics and Research Agency

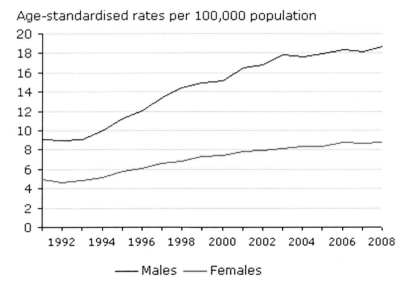

Alcohol-related death rates by sex, United Kingdom, 1991-2008

A Simple 16-Question Quiz designed to help you decide if you have alcohol problem.
- Do you drink because you have problems? To face up to stressful situations?
- Do you drink when you get mad at other people, your friends or parents?
- Do you often prefer to drink alone, rather than with others?
- Are you starting to get low marks? Are you skiving off work?
- Do you ever try to stop or drink less - and fail?
- Have you begun to drink in the morning, before

school or work?
- Do you gulp your drinks as if to satisfy a great thirst?
- Do you ever have loss of memory due to your drinking?
- Do you avoid being honest with others about your drinking?
- Do you ever get into trouble when you are drinking?
- Do you often get drunk when you drink, even when you do not mean to?
- Do you think you're big enough to be able to handle your drinking?
- Do you hide drinks in every corner of your house?
- Do you have a shrine or wine bar in your home?
- Do you have to stop on the highway when police officers pass bye because you think you are above the limit?
- Do you think you will fail police breath test anytime?

The first thing I have come to learn about alcoholism is that it is one of the oldest problems in man's history. Only recently have we begun to benefit from new approaches to the problem. Doctors today, for example, know a great deal more about alcoholism than their predecessors did only two generations ago. They are beginning to define the problem and study it in detail.

While there is no formal unique definition of alcoholism, most of us would agree that, it could be described as a physical compulsion, coupled with a mental obsession. This means we have a distinct physical desire to consume alcohol beyond our capacity to control it, and in defiance of all rules of common sense. We not only have an abnormal craving for alcohol but we frequently yield to it at the worst possible times. We do not know when (or how) to stop drinking and often we do not seem to have sense enough to know when not to begin.

As an alcoholic, you should have learned the hard way that willpower alone, however strong in other respects, is not enough to keep you sober. You have tried going on the wagon for specific periods; you have taken solemn pledges; you have switched brands and beverages; and you have tried drinking only at certain hours, but none of your plans worked. You always wound up, sooner or later, by getting drunk when you only wanted to stay sober and even with every rational incentive to do so.

As cured alcoholics, we have gone through stages of dark despair when we were sure that something was wrong with us mentally. We came to hate ourselves for wasting the talents with which we were endowed and for the trouble we were causing our families and others. Frequently, we indulged in self-pity and proclaimed that nothing could ever help us. We can smile at those recollections now but at the time they were grim, unpleasant experiences. No one in his or her true normal sense and character would have wanted to be like that.

Today we are willing to accept the idea that, as far as we are concerned, alcoholism is an illness, a progressive illness that one can be cured, healed and delivered from but which, like some other illnesses can be arrested also. We agree that there is nothing shameful about having an illness, provided we face the problem honestly and try to do something about it. We are perfectly willing to admit that we are allergic to alcohol and that it is simply common sense to stay away from the source of the allergy.

We understand now that once a person has crossed the

invisible line from heavy drinking to compulsive alcoholic drinking, he may always remain alcoholic. So far as we know, there can never be any turning back to normal social drinking. "Once an alcoholic - always an alcoholic," is a simple fact we have to live with, unless delivered by the mighty hand of God.

We have also learned that there are few alternatives for the alcoholic. If he continues to drink, his problem will become progressively worse; he seems assuredly on the path to the gutter, to hospitals, to jails or other institutions, or to an early grave. The only alternative is to stop drinking completely, to abstain from even the smallest quantity of alcohol in any form. If he is willing to follow this course, and to take advantage of the help available to him, a whole new life can open up for the alcoholic.

The 16 Steps of Help

There is relative and absolute success in the power of God to break the habit and addictive nature of alcoholism. It is a known fact that a former alcoholic has an exceptional faculty for engaging with and helping an uncontrolled drinker, since he has passed that road before. It is good that a recovered alcoholic passes along the story of his or her own drinking problem, describes the sobriety he or she has found in the new alcohol free life, and invites the newcomer to join the informal fellowship of believers.

- Admitted we were powerless over alcohol - that our lives had become unmanageable
- Came to believe that a power greater than ourselves could restore us to sanity
- Made a decision to turn our will and our lives over to the care of God as we understood Him

- Made a searching and fearless moral inventory of ourselves with all sincerity
- Admitted to God, to ourselves and to others the exact nature of our wrongs
- Were entirely ready to have God remove all these defects of character
- Humbly asked God to remove our shortcomings
- Consciously flee from every appearance of evil and alcoholic associations
- Made a list of all persons we had harmed, and became willing to make amends to them all
- Made direct amends to such people wherever possible, except when to do so would injure them or others
- Continued to take personal inventory and when we were wrong promptly admitted it
- Sought through prayer and meditation on the word of God to improve our conscious contact with God as we understood Him, praying only for knowledge of His will for us and the power to carry that out
- Having had a spiritual awakening as the result of these steps, we tried to carry this message to alcoholics and to practice these
- Learnt the habit of daily quiet time and morning devotion with family prayer time as well
- Joined a bible believing church for continued fellowship in prayer and bible studies
- Promised God and relied on Him totally for the rest of our lives

Kiss Me and Go To Hell

A song for the triumphant, alcohol free man

O Jesus, I have promised

1. O Jesus, I have promised
   To serve Thee to the end;
   Be Thou forever near me,
   My Master and my Friend;
   I shall not fear the battle
   If Thou art by my side,
   Nor wander from the pathway
   If Thou wilt be my Guide.

2. Oh, let me feel Thee near me;
   The world is ever near;
   I see the sights that dazzle,
   The tempting sounds I hear;
   My foes are ever near me,
   Around me and within;
   But, Jesus, draw Thou nearer,
   And shield my soul from sin.

3. Oh, let me hear Thee speaking,
   In accents clear and still,
   Above the storms of passion,
   The murmurs of self-will;
   Oh, speak to reassure me,
   To hasten, or control;
   Oh, speak, and make me listen,
   Thou Guardian of my soul.

4. O Jesus, Thou hast promised
   To all who follow Thee
   That where Thou art in glory

There shall Thy servant be;
And Jesus, I have promised
To serve Thee to the end;
Oh, give me grace to follow,
My Master and my Friend.

5. Oh, let me see Thy footmarks,
And in them plant mine own;
My hope to follow duly
Is in Thy strength alone.
Oh, guide me, call me, draw me,
Uphold me to the end;
And then to rest receive me,
My Saviour and my Friend.

19

CLASSIFICATION OF WINES

The classification of wine can be done according to various methods including, but not limited to,

1. By appellation
2. By vinification methods and style
   2.1 Sparkling and still wines
   2.2 Dessert and fortified wine
   2.3 Other styles
3. By vintage or varietal

Practices vary in different countries and regions of origin, and many practices have varied over time. Some classifications enjoy official protection by being part of the wine law in their country of origin, while others have been created by grower's organisations without such protection.

1. *By appellation*

Historically, wines have been known by names reflecting their origin, and sometimes style: Bordeaux, Rioja, Mosel and Chianti are all legally defined names reflecting the traditional wines produced in the named region. These naming conventions or appellations (as they are known in France) reveal not only where the grapes in a wine were grown but also which grapes went into the wine and how they were vinified.

The appellation system is strongest in the European Union, but a related system, the American Viticulture Area, restricts the use of certain regional labels in America, such as Napa Valley, Santa Barbara and Willamette Valley. The AVA designations do not restrict the type of grapes used.

In most of the world, wine labelled Champagne must be made from grapes grown in the Champagne region of France and fermented using a certain method, based on the international trademark agreements included in the 1919 Treaty of Versailles. However, in the United States, a legal definition called semi-generic has enabled U.S. winemakers to use certain generic terms (Champagne, Hock, Sherry, etc.) if there appears next to the term the actual appellation of origin.

More recently, wine regions in countries with less stringent location protection laws such as the United States and Australia have joined with well-known European wine producing regions to sign the Napa Declaration to Protect Wine Place and Origin, commonly known as the Napa Declaration on Place. This is a 'declaration of joint principles stating the importance of location to wine and the need to protect place names'. The Declaration was signed in July 2005 by four United States winegrowing regions and three European Union winegrowing regions.

The signatory regions from the US were Napa Valley, Washington, Oregon and Walla Walla, while the signatory regions from the EU were: Champagne, Cognac (the commune where Cognac wine is produced), Douro (the region where Port wine is produced) and Jerez (the region where Sherry is produced).

The list of signatories to the agreement expanded in March

2007 when Sonoma County, Paso Robles, Chianti Classico, Tokay, Victoria, Australia and Western Australia signed the Declaration at a ceremony in Washington, DC.

2. **By vinification methods and style**

Wines may be classified by vinification methods. These include classifications such as:
- red or white wine,
- sparkling,
- semi-sparkling or still,
- fortified and dessert wines.

The colour of wine is not determined by the juice of the grape, which is almost always clear, but rather by the presence or absence of the grape skin during fermentation. Grapes with colored juice, for example Alicante Bouchet, are known as Teinturier.

Red wine is made from red (or black) grapes, but its red colour is bestowed by a process called maceration, whereby the skin is left in contact with the juice during fermentation. White wine can be made from any colour of grape as the skin is separated from the juice during fermentation. A white wine made from a very dark grape may appear pink or blush. A form of Rosé is called Blanc de Noirs where the juices of red grapes are allowed contact with the skins for a very short time, usually only a couple of hours.

Sparkling and still wines
Sparkling wines such as champagne, contain carbon dioxide which is produced naturally from fermentation or force-injection. To have this effect, the wine is fermented twice, once in an open container to allow the carbon dioxide to escape into

the air, and a second time in a sealed container, where the gas is caught and remains in the wine[7] Sparkling wines that gain their carbonation from the traditional method of bottle fermentation are labelled Bottle Fermented, Méthode Traditionelle, or Méthode Champenoise. The latter designation was outlawed for all wines other than Champagne (which for obvious reasons does not bother to utilise it) in Europe in 1994.

Other international denominations of sparkling wine include Sekt or Schaumwein (Germany), Cava (Spain), and Spumante (Italy).

Semi-sparkling wines are sparkling wines that contain less than 2.5 atmospheres of carbon dioxide at sea level and 20 °C. Some countries such as the UK impose a higher tax on fully sparkling wines. Examples of semi-sparkling synonym terms are Frizzante in Italy, Vino de Aguja in Spain and Petillant in France. In most countries except the United States, champagne is legally defined as sparkling wine originating from a region (Champagne, Towns Reims, Épernay) in France. Still wines are wines that have not gone through the sparkling wine methods and have no effervescence.

Dessert and fortified wine

Dessert wines range from slightly sweet (with less than 50 g/L of sugar) to incredibly sweet wines (with over 400 g/L of sugar). Late harvest wines such as Spätlese are made from grapes harvested well after they have reached maximum ripeness. Dried grape wines, such as Recioto and Vin Santo from Italy as well as Vinsanto from Santorini Greece, are made from grapes that have been partially raisined after harvesting. Botrytised wines are made from grapes infected by the mold Botrytis cinerea or noble rot. These include Sauternes from

Bordeaux, numerous wines from Loire such as Bonnezeaux and Quarts de Chaume, Tokaji Aszú from Hungary and Tokaj from Slovakia, and Beerenauslese from Germany and Austria. Eiswein is made from grapes that are harvested while they are frozen, and are commonly from the Niagara and Okanagan regions in Canada, Germany, and Austria.

Fortified wines are often sweeter, and generally more alcoholic wines that have had their fermentation process stopped by the addition of a spirit, such as brandy, or have had additional spirit added after fermentation. Examples include Port, Madeira and Sherry.

Other styles
Table wines may have an alcohol content that is no higher than 14% in the U.S. In Europe, light wine must be within 8.5% and 14% alcohol by volume. Thus, unless a wine has more than 14% alcohol, or it has bubbles, it is a table wine or a light wine.

Table wines are usually classified as 'white, red, or rosé,' depending on their colour. In Europe 'vins de table' (in French), 'vino da tavola' (in Italian), 'tafelwein' (in German) or 'vino de mesa' (in Spanish), which translate to 'table wine' in English, are cheaper wines that often on the label do not include the information on the grape variety used or the region of origin.

Cooking wine or Cooking sherry refers to inexpensive grape wine or rice wine (in Chinese and other East Asian cuisine). It is intended for use as an ingredient in food rather than as a beverage. Cooking wine typically available in North America is treated with salt as a preservative and food colouring. When a wine bottle is opened and the wine is exposed to oxygen, a

fermentative process will transform the alcohol into acetic acid resulting in wine vinegar. The salt in cooking wine inhibits the growth of the acetic acid producing micro-organisms. This preservation is important because a bottle of cooking wine may be opened and used occasionally over a long period of time.
Cooking wines are convenient for cooks who use wine as an ingredient for cooking rarely. However, they are not widely used by professional chefs, as they believe the added preservative significantly lowers the quality of the wine and subsequently the food made with that wine. Most professional chefs prefer to use inexpensive but drinkable wine for cooking, and this recommendation is given in many professional cooking textbooks as well as general cookbooks. Many chefs believe there is no excuse for using a low quality cooking wine when there are quality drinkable wines available at very low prices.

Cooking wine is considered a wine of such poor quality, that it is unpalatable by itself and intended for use only in cooking. There is a school of thought that advises against cooking with any wine one would find unacceptable to drink[12].

3. By vintage or varietal

A vintage wine is one made from grapes that were all, or primarily, grown in a single specified year, and are accordingly dated as such. Consequently, it is not uncommon for wine enthusiasts and traders to save bottles of an especially good vintage wine for future consumption. However, there is some disagreement and research about the significance of vintage year to wine quality Most countries allow a vintage wine to include a portion of wine that is not from the labelled vintage.
A varietal wine is wine made from a dominant grape such as a Chardonnay or a Cabernet Sauvignon.

The wine may not be entirely of that one grape and varietal labelling laws differ. In the United States a wine needs to be composed of at least 75% of a particular grape to be labelled as a varietal wine. In the European Union, a minimum of 85% is required if the name of a single varietal is displayed, and if two or more varietals are mentioned, these varietals combined must make up 100% and they must be listed in descending order. For example, a mixture of 70% Chardonnay and 30% Viognier must be called Chardonnay-Viognier rather than Viognier-Chardonnay.

Dare Osatimehin

20
ALCOHOL AND WINE

DEFINITIONS

Alcoholic Strength
Natural: from the sugar measured in unfermented grapes or must by a calibrated refractometer or hydrometer and calculated using a conversion table.

Actual: strength of fermented wine, excluding any residual sugar.

Potential: unfermented residual sugar. Definitions of product type - dry, medium dry etc are based on the grams per litre residual sugar in wine.

Total: combined actual and potential alcohol. The reference point for enrichment limits and calculated by converting the residual sugar (grams per litre) to potential alcohol and, adding this to the actual alcohol.

Residual Sugar Labelling Indicators (Still Wine)

Dry: Maximum of 4g/l, or 9g/l where the total acidity content is not more than 2 g/l below the residual sugar content.

Medium Dry: The residual sugar content must exceed the maximum for Dry but not exceed 12g/l or 18g/l where the total acidity content is not more than 10g/l below the residual sugar content.

Medium or Medium Sweet: The residual sugar content must exceed the maximum for Medium Dry but not exceed 45g/l.

Sweet: At least 45g/l.

Note: White wines with a high level of residual sugar and total alcohol exceeding 15% may only be marketed as Quality Wine per Wine Standards Board Guide (WSB)to EU Wine Regulations 7

Sulphur Dioxide
Free: Active SO_2 in the wine. There are minimum and maximum limits for Quality and Regional Wine (see below).

Total Sulphur: Active and Chemically Bound SO_2. Maximum limits depend on residual sugar level in the wine (see below).

Table Wine

Although it is legal to produce wine in the UK using grapes from other EC countries, it is assumed, for the purposes of this book, that wines will only be made using authorised grape varieties grown in the UK. For information about non-UK sourced grapes please consult the WSB.

For wines made from UK grapes, the following criteria must be met:

Alcohol
Minimum natural alcoholic strength for grapes/grape before enrichment - 5% vol.
Minimum actual alcoholic strength - 8.5%vol.
Maximum total alcoholic strength (unenriched wines) - 15% vol.

Fermentation
Yeast nutrients may be added to the must:
Di-ammonium phosphate or ammonium phosphate max - 1.0g/l
Ammonium sulphite/bisulphite max - 0.2g/l

Enrichment
Dry sucrose (cane or beet sugar) is generally used for enrichment in the UK. The quantity of sucrose used must be recorded in winery records. The increase in alcohol must not exceed 3.5% vol. or result in a wine with total alcohol greater than 11.5/12% vol. (white/red). In exceptionally poor years the allowed increase in alcohol may be raised to 4.5% (following industry consultation with Defra and notification to the European Commission) for specified varieties. Grape must or wine may be concentrated through cooling (cryoextraction) provided that:
The volume of wine is not reduced by more than 20%; and,
The natural alcoholic strength is increased by no more than 2% vol.

Record Keeping
The enrichment process must be recorded on the day of operation and notified to the local WSB inspector 48 hours in advance, using form WSB10 (this may be faxed). Forms are provided via an annual mailing to all registered wineries

Control of Oxidation and Active Organisms
By use of gaseous sulphur dioxide or by addition of potassium bisulphite/metabisulphite, subject to maximum levels of total sulphur dioxide:
Red wine 160 mg/litre
White wine 210 mg/litre
Rosé wine 210 mg/litre
Wines with residual sugar - 5 grams/litre:
Red 210 mg/litre
White 260 mg/litre
WSB Guide to EU Wine Regulations 8

Sweetening
Wine may be sweetened with grape (sweet reserve) provided that:
- For enriched wines, the total alcohol of the sweet reserve must not exceed the total alcohol of the finished wine
- For unenriched wines the total alcohol of the finished wine is not increased by more than 2% vol

Sweetening operations must be recorded in winery records, within 24 hours of processing.

De-Acidification
Grape must and new wine may be partially de-acidified, without limit.
Post vintage, using:
Calcium Carbonate (proprietary brands include Acidex and Neo antacid)
Potassium Bicarbonate
Other materials set out in Regulation 1493/1999 Annex IV.1

Other wines may be de-acidified by up to 1g/litre, at any time, but this operation must be notified to the WSB using form WSB14 and recorded in winery records (the form is included in the annual mailing to all registered winemakers).

Filtering/Fining/Gas Blanketing etc
Only the commonly used substances are listed. A full list appears in Regulation 1493/1999, Annex IV.

Wine may be fined using a clarifying agent listed in the Regulations. These include:
- Bentonite
- Gelatine
- Caseinate
- Silicon dioxide (usually as silica sol)
- Isinglass

Stability
Tartrate precipitation in the finished wine may be inhibited by addition of Potassium Bitartrate.

Blending of Wines
Blending of wines is only allowed if it does not involve wines from different categories. The categories are defined as:
- Red must and red wine (including rose wine)
- White must and white wine
- Table wine(including those with geographic descriptors)

Quality wine psr
Blending of wines from the same categories is not allowed if any of the ingredients are illegal e.g. an over-enriched wine (illegal) cannot be blended with an un-enriched or legally enriched wine. However, a table wine that fails to meet the

minimum actual alcoholic strength may be blended with a legal table wine at the premises of the winemaker.

Note: Water is not a permitted additive except as necessary for the dissolution of permitted additives.

WSB Guide to EU Wine Regulations 9
4.4 Sparkling Wine & Quality Sparkling Wine (QSW)
Sparkling wine and quality sparkling wine may be produced in the UK from English and Welsh table wines, as may semi-sparkling wines, aerated sparkling wines and aerated semi-sparkling wines.

Sparkling wines may be produced by any of the traditional production methods: fermentation in sealed vats (curve close method), transfer method, or fermentation in the bottle. In addition, aerated sparkling wines and aerated semi-sparkling wines may be produced by carbonation.

The following requirements must be satisfied:
- Minimum pressure (3 bar; QSW 3.5 bar)
- Sulphur Dioxide (max 235 mg/litre; QSW 185mg/l)
- Alcoholic strength

Actual alcohol (minimum for QSW) 10%
- Total alcohol (minimum)
- Base wine 8.5%
- Base wine (QSW) 9%

Dosage/Tirage
Tirage (to start second fermentation) - max total alcohol increase 1.5%
Dosage (to adjust sweetness of wine) -max total alcohol

increase 0.5%

Semi-Sparkling Wine
Defined as wine with pressure 1-2.5 bar and a minimum actual alcohol of 7% vol.

Quality Sparkling Wine Produced in a Specified Region (psr)
There is currently no provision in the Quality Wine Scheme for the production in the UK of Quality Sparkling Wine psr.

Regional Wine
This is an upper category of Table Wine (equivalent to French Vin de Pays etc).
For the detailed requirements please refer to Table / Regional / Quality Wines - A Summary of the Parameters.

Wines with proven enhanced characteristics are recognized by Defra and are subject to testing and tasting through a system run by the Representative Industry Body (RIB). The RIB is approved by Defra to undertake this task for a fixed period. Presently the RIB function is being performed by the UKVA. Application procedures can be found in the section UKVA Regional Wine Procedures.

Full details are set out in the Defra Notice to Vine Growers and Wine Producers and UKVA information sheets (includes application process, fee and deadlines for tasting dates for the current year) and are included on the WSB web site.

Analysis is either by the designated laboratory or using a Producer's Analysis Certificate. A Tasting Panel is convened by the RIB, or at a UKVA National or Regional Competition, subject to approval by the Secretary of State.

Results are notified by the RIB WSB Guide to EU Wine Regulations 10

Quality Wine

Full details of Quality Wine production requirements and application procedures are given in the Defra "Notice to Vine Growers and Wine Producers."

Production Requirements
Alcohol:
Enrichment: Wines may be enriched up to 3.5%, with no upper total alcohol limit. However wines which fail quality wine application will only be allowed to be marketed on application to the WSB, usually as Table Wine.

Free Sulphur Dioxide:
Minimum 15mg/l (a lower level is permitted only if 'effective oenological techniques' have been used or for dry wines meeting additional specified criteria) Maximum 45mg/l for dry wines.

Total Sulphur Dioxide:
Wines described as "botrytis" or similar are allowed a higher maximum level of 300 mg/l.

Sweetening:
Quality Wine may only be sweetened with sweet reserve sourced in the quality wine region.

A PRAYER OF SALVATION

A born-again, committed relationship with God is the key to the victorious life. Jesus laid down his life and rose again so that we could spend eternity with Him in heaven and experience His absolute best on earth. If you would like to receive Jesus into your life in order to become born again, pray this prayer from your heart:

Heavenly Father, I come to you admitting that I am a sinner. Right now, I choose to turn away from sin, and I ask You to cleanse me of all unrighteousness. I believe that Your Son Jesus died on the cross to take away my sins. I also believe that He rose again from the dead so that I might be justified and made righteous through faith in Him. I call upon the name of Jesus Christ to be the Saviour and Lord of my life. Jesus, I choose to follow You and ask that You fill me with the power of the Holy Spirit. I declare that right now I am a child of God. I am free form sin and full of the righteousness of God. I am saved in Jesus' name amen.

Romans 10:8-11
V.8 But what saith it? The word is nigh thee, even in thy mouth, and in thy heart: that is, the word of faith, which we preach
V.9 that if thou shalt confess with thy mouth the Lord Jesus, and shalt believe in thy heart that God hath raised him from the dead, thou shalt be saved
V.10 For with the heart man believeth to righteousness; and with the mouth confession is made to salvation

V.11 for the scripture saith, whoever believeth on him shall not be ashamed.

If you have prayed this prayer to receive Jesus Christ as your Saviour or if this book has changed your life, I would like to hear from you. Please write to:

Total word publishing
815 Dagenham Road
Dagenham
Essex
RM10 7UP
England

You can also visit www.totalword.co.uk
Or call +44 (o)7946643554

Bible Abbreviations

Gen – Genesis

Num – Numbers

Lev – Leviticus

Deut – Deuteronomy

Chron – Chronicles

Neh – Nehemiah

Prov – Proverbs

Eccl – Ecclesiastes

Jer – Jeremiah

Hab – Habakkuk

Zeph – Zepheniah

Zech - Zechariah

Matt – Matthew

Cor - Corinthians

Tim – Timothy

Gal – Galatians

Eph – Ephesians

Phil – Philippians

Col – Colossians

Thess – Thessalonians

Tim – Timothy

Rev - Revelation

ABOUT THE AUTHOR

Dr. Dare Osatimehim is the Pastor of Total Word Bible Ministries, London. Since his conversion to Christianity in 1984, he has served under various ministries locally and internationally. He started Total Word Bible Ministries after over twenty years as an armour bearer to other churches.

Dare teaches the word of God with simplicity and practicality. A man of praying power, healing and deliverance, his dogged determination to know more of God and defend the Faith makes him an outstanding contemporary teacher of the Bible.

He is a man of only one book, the Bible; happily married and blessed with three wonderful children.

ANOTHER BOOK BY THE AUTHOR
Basketful of Fragments

Basketful of fragments is a simple, systematic and expository study of doctrines of the Christian faith.

- It presents a logical and simplified step-by-step self-study of the Christian Faith.
- It makes you dig a little deeper into God's word.
- It presents topics such as the Bible, Faith, Prayer, Sanctification, Evangelism, Marriage, Tithe in a study format.
- It's a systematic approach to Escathological studies.
- It's a must-have book for all lovers of God.
- Study a chapter in a week and become a full stature Christian in a year.